IN

MW01502646

HERBERT V. COULTON

Photo by Peggy E. C. Lee

With James Daniely

Llumina Press

ISBN: 978-1-60594-441-8

Printed in the United States of America by Llumina Press

Library of Congress Control Number: 2009913281

Contents

Acknowledgements i

Foreword: Rev. Wyatt T. Walker iii

Introduction: James G. Daniely v

Chapter 1: The Early Years (1934-61) 1

Chapter 2: SCLC & Maxcine Bullock 15

Chapter 3: A New Career: Beyond SCLC 51

Chapter 4: The Church 57

Chapter 5: Majoring in Minors 65

Chapter 6: Appointments 71
And Some Thoughts on Virginia's Governors

Chapter 7: Unsung Heroes 79

Epilogue... 99

Bibliography 103

Photos 107

Acknowledgements

This is the 75th year of my life and I started this book 29 years ago. My wife, Maxcine said, "With all that you have been through, you need to write a book." I agreed and sat down and wrote about 19 pages and stopped. Every time she would see me writing something she would ask, "Have you started back on your book?" I would answer, "I am not motivated to continue."

It was not until she and my son's godfather, Dr. Joseph Cooper, jointly said to me again, "You need to pen some of those experiences" that something happened.

Soon after that, my friend Dr. James Daniely, Director of United Campus Ministry, asked if he could begin to tape record me speaking about aspects of my life. At that point, I heard the voice of reason because these coincidences could not be explained away.

I have been blessed beyond measure. Hopefully, you will understand how family, friends, and my faith have sustained me and empowered me to do what I do. If this book is about anything, it demonstrates that God is real and will ultimately reward those willing to stay the course.

To those persons who have inspired me, supported me, or prayed for me; to all those persons who have encouraged me or enlightened me, I acknowledge you with heart felt gratitude and love.

However, I dedicate this book to my wife of 45 years, Maxcine Bullock Coulton; my son, born in the struggle, Herbert V. Coulton, Jr.; and my grandchildren: Brittany, Tadia, and Jalen.

Foreword

Wyatt T. Walker

I am delighted to have the opportunity to write this foreword for Herbert V. Coulton. During my tenure as Pastor of the historic Gillfield Baptist Church in Petersburg, Virginia, I met Herb when he was just a lad in the equally historic First Baptist Church of that city. Even as a youth, I was impressed with his polite, yet serious demeanor. In fact, Herbert Coulton was an early pioneer with us in Southside, Virginia. He came into his manhood as the Southern cauldron of the now famous civil rights movement began to boil.

First with our NAACP youth work and very soon thereafter with the newly formed Petersburg Improvement Association, Herb was intricately involved. He supported our assault on the Petersburg Public Library, picketed with us against segregation at lunch counters, and participated in the very difficult task of voter registration to which the hated poll tax frustrated our efforts.

However daunting the task, Herb was always in the front line of volunteers for human rights. His spirit is cast in the mold of our pioneers, Frederick Douglas and W.E. B. DuBois. When the call came for me to join Martin Luther King, Jr. in Atlanta with the Southern Christian Leadership Conference (SCLC), the Petersburg movement could not have survived without Herbert Coulton standing strong with my colleagues of the struggle, Milton A. Reid and Robert G. Williams.

As the sinews and muscles of SCLC expanded in the Deep South our staff needs began to grow. Dr. King, aware that Virginia was strategic in our struggle, asked me, "Wyatt, who can we put to work in Virginia?" I answered, "I know just the man, Herbert Coulton!" The rest is history. Herbert helped SCLC to become the dominant and leading Civil Rights organization of that era. He coordinated Dr. King's *People to*

People tour in several Virginia cities. It was his untiring work that brought to life the first state conference of SCLC affiliates. It was Herbert who put together the mass rally at Virginia State University's Rogers Stadium in 1965, where Dr. King made his first pronouncement against the war in Vietnam. He has been a stout soldier across the years and continues to allow his beacon to shine.

The social and political climates, as well as the demographics, of the South were changed in revolutionary fashion with the passage of the *1964 Public Accommodations* bill and the *1965Voting Rights Act.* It should be known that Herbert Coulton's fingerprints are on both bills. It has been persons like Herbert Coulton, unsung heroes, who did the grunt work that made the movement of the 1960's an international cause to celebrate.

When America's interests and priorities cooled on Black issues, Herbert remained on the firing line. The glamour of the struggle of the early 1960's faded with the rise of Richard Nixon, but Herbert Coulton did not fade. He has remained in the thick of the battle for human dignity as his vocation and avocation. Herb, you have been an integral part of my life and I, along with every one in the Commonwealth of Virginia, am grateful.

Introduction

James G. Daniely

How does one re-call a great chapter in the life and struggle of a nation to become whole? In examining the heroes, their accomplishments, and their humanity, how does one capture their courage? How does an outsider, from another generation, appreciate the immensity of a struggle that he's only read about? Admittedly, I am only a generation removed from the Civil Rights Struggle, but the distance cannot be measured in years alone. I need to look beneath the surface and take a look at the hearts of persons willing to risk everything for a dream.

In addition, we need the connecting stories of local heroes, giants among their peers, who connected the regions, state by state, and made a national movement possible. This is not to take anything away from the established national advocates; i.e., Dr. Martin L. King, Dr. Joseph Lowery, Dr. Wyatt T. Walker, or the Rev. Jesse Jackson. Instead, it is my intent to demonstrate not only that Herbert V. Coulton was a major contributor to the establishment of the Virginia Chapter of the SCLC, hence embodying the movement in his very being, but also that he is a living hero of the first magnitude among Americans in general and African Americans in particular.

Therefore, his story does not begin nor end with the Civil Rights struggle. Herb was, and is, a renaissance man, a person who transcends his environment and elevates those around him. Although the movement perhaps refined the man, it did not and cannot, define the man.

I met Mr. Coulton in the mid 1990's, while I was serving at Virginia State University, and have maintained a friendship with him over these many years. Beginning in the summer of 2007, we taped several hours of interviews and then began gathering materials and verifying dates of events, to ensure the integrity of this work. In addition, I sought out persons still living to add their impressions of events and photo documentation of as many events as possible. As a result, our collaboration is offered to posterity as a historical deposit, sharing a glimpse into the life of a great human being, a child of the Most High God whose ancestry was scorched by the African sun and then transported to these shores.

I want to thank Ms. Evelyn Green and Ms. Lili Spain-Daniely for their tireless efforts in editing this work. Without their careful reading and correction of my errors, this work would not be what it is today.

Yet ultimately, this work is about Herb Coulton and it is his story we're attempting to tell. His life embodies struggle, the desire to claim the possibilities available in God for all of God's people.

So as we work to complete our task, we see another beam of light cast by Herb's shadow, the historic election of Barack H. Obama, which has added another spectrum to his work. For you see, there were many people who called him and personally thanked him for making it possible. Why Herb? Because he not only believed in the impossible, he worked tirelessly for it and passed it on to others. That's my story, and I'm sticking to it.!

Chapter 1:

The Early Years

"I was young and now I am old, yet I have never seen the righteous forsaken or their children begging bread."
Psalm 37:25 (NIV)

My mother, Mrs. Nettie Brown Coulton, showed here in a picture probably one year or so before my birth. This photo is the only known image of my mother and has been a treasured possession for many years.

Before I begin my story, I want to say something about my mother, whom I never knew. Nettie Brown Coulton was born in Prince George County on March 26, 1902. (In order to validate my information, I went to the Health Department in 1951 and received a copy of her death certificate on which also listed her birth date and this confirmed my information). She died from pneumonia, which today, with the right medication and bed rest, she might have recovered to nurture and care for us. It was only after my mother's sister, Aunt Corrine, came to visit us when I was around 6 or 7, that I found out she was actually dead. Her words, "What a pity that 'sister' died and left these young children'" hit me like a ton of bricks. Perhaps my dad thought we were too young to understand death but I never recall him talking about her either. He would respond to specific questions that my older siblings asked, but I think it pained him to talk about her.

As a child, I used to hear the song entitled, "Motherless Child." The words went like this: "A motherless child has a mighty hard time when mother is gone." I never really paid much attention… then. I haven't heard the song in years…but its sentiment haunts me. Daddy used to sing it and I never thought to ask, "Where is my mother?" I am sure that she hugged and kissed me as an infant, but I never experience it as a child; never got to call her 'Mother' or experience a Mother's Day with her. So for many years, on Mother's Day, as flowers were being given to mothers for various reasons, my tear ducts would overflow. I even recall asking, "God, Why did you take my mother away?" There were many moments of anger and sadness; but with much prayer God removed them from me! Yes, I know it was selfish on my part, but I really wish I had the chance to have known her, to at least call her, Mother!

"To one who has the sweetest name,
And adds a luster to the same.
To one who cheers when I am sad,
The greatest friend I've ever had.
Long life to her, for there's no other
To take the place of my dear mother."

(Author unknown)

It was the Great Depression and times were hard. Franklin D. Roosevelt was President and the recovery from the Stock

Market crash was in full blast, even in Virginia. A new house cost $5,972.00, the average income was $1,601/ year, a new automobile was $625.00, and the average rent was $20.00/month. In addition, a movie ticket was $.25; gasoline was $.10/gallon, and postage stamps, $.03. Food was also very inexpensive. For example, ground coffee cost $.35/pound, bacon about $.25/pound, eggs were $.17/dozen, and a loaf of bread was $.08. My father, Richard Coulton, was working for the WPA (Works Program Administration, a federal program designed to help young people get jobs) and was paid $.17/hour. Poverty had a grip on Black America and the political machines stymied our efforts to better ourselves. Yet, we had hope.

Into this era of hope, I was born in April of 1934 on Bollingbrook Street, near Third Street and almost across the street from Miss Lola Johnson, who would be one of my sixth grade teachers. This house belonged to my great Aunt, Cora Moore, and portions of my extended family lived there as well. When I was just three weeks old, my mother, Nettie Brown Coulton, died leaving my father (Richard James Coulton) with four small children to take care of, the best he could. At the time my brother (Marvin Wilbert) was 3 years old, my sister (Francis Adelle) was 5 and my oldest brother (Richard Eldridge) was 8 years old. Some men would have given up or farmed out the children, but my daddy was not having it. When asked by his sisters to at least allow them to take the two smaller ones, he told them "all of them are mine and I'm going to take care of them the best I can." After getting a raise to $.22/hour, Daddy hired a lady, Miss Marie, to take care of us during the day and went off to his job making less than $10.00/week!

We all lived on Bollingbrook Street (house now torn down) until I was almost 5 years old. After that daddy and his sister, Adelle, were forced to move. We went to Old Church St. and Aunt Adelle went to Crater Road. From what I was told, that house on Bollingbrook was pretty nice and when I think about it, had to be of sufficient size to accommodate all of us.

Aunt Cora owned other property in Prince George County as well, but in a scene reminiscent of many played out in the South involving poor blacks and property, she lost it. She was illiterate, and because she did not know to pay the taxes nor was willing to trust family members to help her, she was scammed. When she received the tax notices, rather than seek someone from the neighborhood like a teacher or the minister to explain what the notices meant, she trusted a local white man. This man told her not to worry about the notices and that if more came in, he would take care of the matter. Well he took care of them all right. After the third notice, this person paid the taxes, claimed the properties, and made Aunt Cora move. The larger property was sold to the government and I believe, later became a part of Camp Lee (now named Fort Lee).

However, by that time, Aunt Cora was old, broke and had moved to Crater Road to stay with Aunt Adelle. She was very fond of me, and I of her, so I moved to Crater Road with her and slept at the foot of her bed. My other siblings were with daddy on Old Church Street, but it would not be long before we were all back together again. Aunt Cora died that year, 1939, and I went home to be with my family.

Though he never told us, I'm sure that daddy loved us. He was no nonsense kind of fellow, probably what we would call now, 'tough love'. So he didn't play! I was told that he quit school because they had recess. Now I don't know if that was the real reason, but he did drop out of school in the 4th grade. Yet he washed our clothes, ironed them, and sewed them when needed, prepared our meals and helped us with our homework. I still marvel at what he did and wonder how he managed it all.

Ted Cook, in defining parents, has this to say, "Parents are people who spend half their time worrying how a child will turn out and the rest of the time wondering when a child will turn in." Daddy saw that we turned in, because we never went out. We were called "yard birds" because we stayed in our yard. He bought us some boxing gloves and horseshoes from

Montgomery Ward to keep us busy and we were content. Every day, when Miss Marie allowed us to go outside, we played sock ball, horseshoes, and boxed until we were either tired or it was time to come in.

When I grew older and was attending Peabody High School, I got a job delivering newspapers. **Floyd Henderson**, a childhood friend (later to become the Principal at both Robert E. Lee & Walnut Hill Elementary schools), **Orriss "Jake " Powell** and **William Pegram** carried the *Progress Index* (they had bicycles) and I, in my wagon, carried the black papers -*The Afro*, *Journal & Guide*, *Pittsburg Courier*, and *Chicago Defender*. At that time, daddy could not afford a bicycle for me so I had to use what was available. Yet, we went throughout Blandford to most of the blacks. The whites had their own paperboys and that was just how things were-separate, but unequal.

I served many customers with my black newspapers all over Blandford. I remember that when I attended Mrs. Florence Gills 100th birthday at the Hopewell Health Care Center, it was like a re-union of sorts. I saw many of the same people I had delivered newspapers to as a young adult and I bet many of them still owed me money after more than 50 years. I did not want the money, but it sure was good to see them again after so many years.

I graduated from Peabody in 1951 and immediately got a job at the Petersburg Hotel as a Hall Boy. I was wondering why it was so easy to get that job and then I received my first check and understood perfectly: they weren't paying very much. I asked Mr. Morgan, the owner of the Petersburg Hotel, for a loan and thought being honest in telling him I wanted to go to college would have impressed him. The words were hardly out of my mouth before he told me emphatically, "no." He wasn't even sorry, just no! College tuition wasn't very much but I needed additional clothes, just the bare necessities.

Petersburg Hotel, like many establishments of the time permitted only white customers, but all the workers- maids, bellhops, cooks, and waiters- were black and underpaid. At this time, Petersburg had no motels and only two other small hotels, but the Petersburg Hotel was where the 'movers and shakers' met, the people who ran the city. The Lions, Kiwanis, and the Rotary Clubs held regular meetings there and Floyd Henderson and I served as waiters every Tuesday, Wednesday, and Thursday. We each earned $2.00 per meeting and gleaned several matters that would serve us well as we went into the wider world. For example, we were introduced to parliamentary procedures, which have helped both of us as God has elevated us to various leadership roles.

In the fall of 1952, I enrolled in the Industrial Education Department at Virginia State College (VSC, now VSU). Although it was not what I really wanted or where I would ultimately finish, I began my higher education with a tailoring course. Mr. T. D. Lane was the instructor and when grades were posted, I had earned a passing grade. This really lifted me and filled me with a deep sense of pride because I felt I had accomplished one of my goals: to be enrolled at VSC!

The next summer, I went to Salisbury, MD and worked at the Campbell Soup Company. In the fall of '53, I was back at VSC and began my studies in Elementary Education. I did well and continued the following year. However, the second half of my junior year, I didn't have the money and could not borrow any money to continue so I went to see the Treasurer, Mr. James Cephas. He kept telling me to come back and he'd see what he could do. Dr. A. G. Macklin, my Personal and Social Adjustment professor, told me to keep on coming to campus and to 'bug' Mr. Cephas. In fact, Dr. Macklin said, "Go every day if you have to." Well I went back every day and in fact many students thought I was still enrolled. But each time it was the same old story, "Come back tomorrow." In my spirit I felt he was not going to help me, even though he never said so. I just felt that I had done all that I could and he was not going to give me the money to enroll. So, after awhile, I stopped going.

As much as I wanted to go to college, this could have devastated me but I could not stay down. In the back of my mind, I could still hear the poem I had learned in high school by Langston Hughes,

Mother To Son:

"Well Son, I'll tell you: life for me ain't been no crystal stair. It's had tacks in it, and splinters, and boards torn up, and places with no carpet on the floor-bare. But all the time I'se been a-climbin' on, and reachin' landin's and turnin' corners, and sometimes goin' in the dark where there ain't been no light. So boy, don't you turn back. Don't you set down on the steps 'Cause you find it's kinder hard. Don't you fall now- For I'se still goin', honey. I'se still climbing And life for me ain't been no crystal stair."[1]

I could have taken to drinking but I didn't like the taste of liquor or beer. I could have felt sorry for myself or become irritated, but instead I got smart. And although the Korean War was just off the front pages, I answered the draft in March 1957. So it's off to basic training for me, along with George Washington and Oscar "Dickie Boy" Thurman. George was a high school classmate and "Dickie Boy" and I used to play on the playgrounds and school grounds of Blandford. Basic training was a snap for me. Compared to my daddy, those drill sergeants were mild.

My daddy should have been a drill sergeant since he had acted like one all of my life. For example, even though I was advancing toward full manhood, I was still required to be in the house by 10:30 p.m. I mean all my siblings had moved out, it was just the two of us in the house, but he would not relent. He was working the night shift at Norfolk and

[1] From Selected Poems copyright 1959 by Langston Hughes. Published by Alfred A. Knopt, Inc.

Western Railroad by now and I had to be home before he went to work. I became angry, and kept it to myself, but it would not have made a difference. Finally, I accepted the fact that it was his house and that he had the right to set the rules. After dealing with him all of my life, the drill sergeants were 'a piece of cake'.

While at Ft. Jackson, I was very pleased to be near my elder brother Richard who was on the staff at South Carolina State College, serving in the R.O.T.C. Department. When I had the time, he or his wife, Emma, would pick me up on Friday night and allow me to stay with them in Orangeburg until Sunday. This was a great get-away for me and helped me to renew my relationship with my brother, who had been gone from Petersburg for about six years.

One week, they said they were going away to see our Aunt Corrine Jackson, my mother's sister, who lived in Philadelphia. Yet they still wanted me to take advantage of their place, to come away from the Post, using the Greyhound Bus as my transportation. Well, I did so and thinking that I knew the schedule, planned my stay to the very last minute. Thinking that the last bus from Orangeburg departed at midnight, I arrived at the station at 11:45 p.m. When the agent told me that the last bus had already departed (at 11:00 p.m.), a sinking feeling came over me. Although the distance to Columbia was only 44 miles, it might as well have been a million. All I could think about was missing reveille (the first military formation of the day) and the fact that my Company had never had anyone miss it! Now that's one record that I did not want the distinction of breaking, so I made up my mind to walk.

As I began the walk to Columbia, I was wearing a Sear Sucker suit with an open neck, short sleeve shirt, a straw hat, and some shoes that were good to look at, but not made for walking long distances. I knew that if I were to get back to the Post on time, I'd need some luck; things would have to work just right. So, I began to run since I was in pretty good shape.

Running in those shoes was not the wisest thing I could have done, so when my feet started to hurt, I walked. As cars approached, I would put out my thumb, but no luck. Now remember that it's 1957 and I am in the Deep South, at night walking along a semi-deserted road. Not many people would stop to give a black man a ride. I began to think about the possibility that I might not make it as a few 'good ole boys' went by with shotguns in the back of their trucks. My heart was racing and I was sweating profusely. The mosquitoes seemed to be a big as horseflies and they were having a good time feeding on me. But I kept on walking.

By the time I saw the sign saying, "Columbia, 13 miles," I had gotten rid of my straw hat. Then, because my shirt was soaking wet, I threw away my jacket! As I continued to walk, my belt even became heavy and I got rid of it also! It was still dark at 4:05 a.m. when an old white fellow in a late model car pulled over. I said, "Sir, I need to get to Fort Jackson by 4:45 a.m. and I am willing to pay if you will take me." Something in him was moved as he responded, "Young man, I am not going to Fort Jackson but you look like you really need to get there, so I'll take you." Of course I thanked him several times but you have no idea how grateful I was. I arrived at the Post at 4:39, took a quick shower, changed clothes, and made it to my formation on time. That was a scary moment for me but looking back, I believe that God allowed that man to come my way.

When we finished basic training at Fort Jackson, twenty-five of us were assigned to Hawaii. There were 13 white and 12 black soldiers traveling together and for some reason, the Sergeant gave the meal tickets to me. I have often wondered about this because none of us had any rank, so why did I get the tickets? Well when we arrived at Atlanta, after my first ever flight, a pivotal chapter in my life began to unfold.

In those days, the airport at Atlanta was not a first class facility. However it did have a cafeteria, and that's where we were supposed to eat. We went into the cafeteria and the headwaiter, a black man, stopped us. He said, "You white boys go ahead inside and take a seat. You colored boys, wait until I can get a black board that you will have to sit behind." Something in me was offended by that attitude. And since I had the meal tickets, I spoke up. "We are not sitting behind some black board," I said angrily. I don't know if my anger was stimulated more by his words or his ready acceptance of the status quo, but I was irritated. "It's the law," he said. "Then, we won't eat here," I replied. The white soldiers said, "We're hungry Herb, give the man the damn tickets!" "If we have to eat behind that black board, then we will not eat here," was my reply. One of them said, "You know, we can beat you up and take the tickets." Without missing a beat, I replied with perfect determination, "You could beat me up, but on my way down, I'll tear these meal tickets up." The black soldiers saw what was at stake and came to my defense saying, "You won't be beating on Herb today, not as long as we are standing here"! Looking back, that was my entrée into the movement for freedom and change. I did not think so at the time, but with hindsight, that was the moment I stood up and have not stop standing since.

Now when we arrived in Hawaii, we were assigned to the Army Camp called Scofield Barracks. And not long after that, the Commanding Officer (CO) sent for me. When I reported, he said to me, "Soldier, you are in trouble. We are going to court martial you." My heart began to race, but I responded, "Sir, what are the charges?" he said, "You refused to allow the soldiers to eat in Atlanta." My reply was not intended to be smart, but some would say it came out that way. "Sir, I didn't stop them from eating. We were paid before we left Ft. Jackson and if they wanted to, they could have used their own money to eat." But the CO was getting red in the face and responded, "Oh, you are one of those smart ones. You were issued meals tickets and you would not let them use them. What do you have to say about that?" Now, I am getting mad, but I cannot show it and a strange calm comes over me. "Sir, if the same thing would happen today, I would respond in the same way ," I said. He was livid and shouted at me, "Report back to your unit, we'll get you later!" Well, it's been over 50 years, and I have not heard from that CO about that matter yet.

But I don't want you to think that we were experiencing paradise in Hawaii, as it is often described. No, it was still the 1950's and racial tensions were the same there as everywhere else. My CO was always talking about "Niggras"(sic) sitting next to his mother in Georgia and our 1st Sgt. shared that he had received letters from his sister saying, '"Niggras" (sic) were trying to sit by her and that he might have to take some leave so that he could go home and take some target practice." They knew we did not hear these tacit remarks as humorous statements; yet the same words or similar ones, were being repeated in the barracks, the Orderly Room, and even the cafeteria. So although we were sharing the same quarters, we were a divided Camp. I knew at that moment that I would join any organization that would take a stand against these racist, oppressive attitudes.

I was discharged in 1959 and returned to Petersburg. I saw that the biggest step that Blacks could make is that short walk to the ballot box. Therefore, I began to organize in Blandford early in the same year. I purchased index cards and began canvassing the neighborhood in an attempt to get the names of everybody in the Community.

Fear had been instilled in our hearts by repeated acts of intimidation over many generations and it was the largest obstacle for me to overcome. Many persons were afraid to give me their names. I explained who I was, what I was attempting to do, but they were still afraid. I was not affiliated with any organization at the time and that only increased their paranoia. But I knew what I was doing was a step in the right direction and hence I continued until people began to read about and see images of the Movement in other places. When they saw their brothers and sisters in the Deep South standing up, they were motivated and recognized that 'the vote' was important to change things.

By August of 1959, I was employed at Central State Hospital, a segregated facility funded by the Commonwealth of Virginia. And although most of the patients were blacks, all the managers were whites. There were two cafeterias, one for whites and one for blacks. I wanted to picket the white cafeteria, but none of the blacks would join me. They were afraid of losing their jobs. So instead, we began picketing the Blue Ribbon Market on Halifax Street.

Although the owners of the establishment were white, most of their financial support came from the black community. We asked them to hire more blacks and at least one black cashier. They refused and we began to protest their hiring practices! Someone from Central State took pictures of the demonstrators, enlarged them in order to identify the persons, and I was identified as one of the marchers holding a picket sign. The Office of Human Resources called me in for a chat. Their position was that since Central State was a state institution, what I was doing was not in line with their understanding of state law. Therefore, they asked me to consider refraining from picketing. My position was that I worked whenever I was scheduled to. I gave them 8 hours each day, what I did with the other 16 was my business. I wanted to be involved in this movement of change and there was nothing illegal about it. Management told me, "Well, you can go back to work now, but you'll hear from us later." I stayed on that job for two and a half years, until February of 1962, and never heard another word about my activities.

In the process of time, our demonstrations forced the Blue Ribbon Market out of business. People did not want to cross our picket line, and since they would not change their policy, people stopped shopping there. As this result unfolded, we saw the value of this tool and began to utilize it elsewhere.

There were several establishments that we targeted and began protests against, all while I was working for Central State by the way, but none more worthwhile than our involvement with Petersburg General Hospital. We repeatedly met with the Administrator, Mr. George Bokinsky, who always insisted that he was doing all he could do. But their policy of relegating blacks to a portion of the second floor left a bad taste in all of our mouths. Not only that, but the rooms were gloomy because the draperies were worn and often dirty. Whenever an inspection team was dispatched in response to our complaints, the hospital's administration was notified at least a week in advance, thereby giving them time to rectify matters. They would move patients and beds around, hang clean draperies, and make the units very presentable. It was always our hope that they, the inspectors, would just once come unannounced and see what the hospital was really like.

Often, tragedy can be a stimulus for change and we thought this was the case later that year. **Mrs. Eva Jackson**, a member of First Baptist Church, had a heart attack during an evening worship service. Our Pastor, **Rev. Milton Reid**, left the pulpit, with his robe on, and assisted Mrs. Jackson to the hospital. He contacted her doctor and pleaded with him to get her a room at Petersburg General because the emergency room staff told us, "We have no space for her." Her doctor, Dr. Charles Townes, would not even make the attempt because he had been refused before. But Rev. Reid was adamant because he felt that Mrs. Jackson might die while being transported to Richmond. Still the hospital would not budge from their position and, fortunately, Mrs. Jackson did not die as a result of their racial policies. However most of us felt an opportunity to integrate Petersburg General was lost.

Chapter 2:

The Southern Christian Leadership Conference & Maxcine Bullock

"Now the Lord is the Spirit, and where the Spirit of the Lord is there is freedom." (II Corinthians 3:17NIV)

From left: David Gunter, Hermanze Fauntleroy, Martin King, and myself, Herbert Coulton, at the Byrd (Richmond, VA) Airport 1965. (In the background is Hulon Willis.) This photo is a part of my personal collection of my time with SCLC.

So after getting my feet wet, so to speak, I heard about this preacher who "was shaking things up." His name: **The Rev. Wyatt T. Walker**. He would go into pool halls, with his robe on, and often stand around and speak with the brothers on the avenue. We saw it as visiting with "the least, the lost, and the left out." And it was the talk of the town because no one had ever heard of a minister doing such things. I recall seeing him a couple of times myself and his actions motivated me to do more. We had not joined forces together but our mission was the same and soon our paths would intertwine. In fact, after he led a march down to the Library to insist upon its integration and was arrested, my voter registration activities were easier. People began believing that perhaps this is the time and begun to find the resources to pay their illegal poll taxes.

On **March 6, 1960**, I attended my first Mass meeting at Zion Baptist Church. Zion had never had that many people before, or since! We were packed in every inch of the pews, the balcony was full, and people were standing against the walls. Excitement was in the air and could not be quenched; not even by the arrests that evening. More than 30 persons were arrested, including Rev. Walker, and **Mr. William M. Bland, Sr.,** owner of Bland's Funeral Home, bailed them all out of jail.

Rev. Walker had articulated our voice but the word on the street was that he was leaving to go to accept a position in Atlanta offered by **Dr. Martin L. King, Jr**. I did not want him to go. Little did I know that it was fortuitous for both of us. Prior to his leaving, he called me and said he was in fact leaving but hoped that I would one day join him in Atlanta. He believed that SCLC would be enlarging its staff and that he was aware of the work I was doing. Accompanying him to Atlanta was **Jim Wood** and **Dorothy Cotton**, both of whom were employees at VSU.

I continued to work with voter registration and the newly formed **Petersburg Improvement Association (PIA)** as we intensified our work for change in Petersburg. As we approached the segregated infrastructure of Petersburg, we developed a threefold strategy of *investigation*, *negotiation*, and if that did not work, *demonstration*. Most people who have accepted the system of segregation have never come to grips with the rightness of wrongness of it. And therefore they have not considered the damage it does to the souls and minds of black people, children and adults alike. So in a real sense, this was a battle for the soul of America, black folks and white folks alike.

All of the "five and dime stores" (W.T. Grant, Woolworth, Kressge), the clothing stores, the movies, Liberty Market, High's Ice Cream Store, and even the Trailway Bus Station practiced overt discrimination. They would not negotiate with us and were therefore picketed. Some of the businesses were extremely adamant against change and one in particular, **Globe Department Store** was on record saying, "I'd rather close than allow a nigger in these doors!" Well, Globe is closed and so is **Spyros**, another blatant discriminator. Although it is also closed now, it should be mentioned that **Mollock's Clothing Store** was a shining, beacon of hope. Not only did they hire a black salesperson, they attempted to assist in other ways. When students from either Peabody or VSC had their clothing ripped or torn during a demonstration, Mollock's would provide free clothing to replace what they had lost. We wanted to be included in the work force where we spent our money and people fought us to prevent it from becoming a reality. But the spirit of freedom was in the air and would not be denied.

Meeting Dr. Martin Luther King, Jr.

Finally, in **January 1962**, I received a letter from the new Executive Director of SCLC, Rev. Wyatt T. Walker, inviting me to come to Atlanta. He said the SCLC was ready to expand their staff and specifically was looking for Field Secretaries. I was to come for an interview with Dr. King and the letter included a round trip ticket.

I began to get excited as the plane touched down in Atlanta. A car was waiting for me and I was taken to the SCLC office where I met with Rev. Walker. He introduced me to Ms. Dora

McDonald, Dr. King's secretary, and I was told by her, "Dr. King will be with you shortly." Man, was I nervous! Here I am, a poor boy from Blandford, about to have a private conversation and an interview with a living legend, the Rev. Dr. Martin L. King, Jr. Now, I really was excited!

When Ms. McDonald finally said, "Dr. King will see you now," all of my nerves were settled and the calmness, which came over me, had to be from God. I felt like I was doing what God had intended for me all along and somehow, I was right where God had intended for me to be, at the exact moment I was supposed to be there. Have you ever had a moment like that where you felt or understood that you were aligned with a Divine Plan? Well, that's the only way I can attempt to get you to understand what was happening inside of me at that moment.

However, stepping into the office, I expected plush surroundings, overstuffed chairs, and the like. But it was not to be. It was a simplistic setting, as non-pretentious as the man who greeted me with a warm smile and an out-stretched hand. Here I was, face to face with a living legend and he was just as humble as I had hoped he would be. His warm demeanor and those first words really caught me off guard, "Herbert Coulton, I've heard so many nice things about you that I have but one question for you." Now, I am thinking, "I sure hope I have the answer!" But his smile put me at ease and the question was, "When can you begin with us?" Rev. Walker had already convinced him that I was the man for Virginia and I will always be indebted to him. I left Atlanta with a deep sense of purpose and a new job title, **Field Secretary for VA**. I came home and continued to work, leading demonstrations and conducting Voter Registration, but also building coalitions.

It was apparent, by then, that no one organization could perform all the tasks necessary and that we had to work together in order to be effective in our work toward freedom. Someone suggested that we have a Mass Meeting in Petersburg and **David Gunther**, President of the Petersburg Improvement

Association, **Rev. Curtis Harris**, President of the Hopewell Improvement Association, worked with me and my pastor, **Dr. Milton A. Reid**, State President S.C.L.C., to make it happen. We worked diligently and when I was able to get a confirmation that my boss, Dr. Martin Luther King, Jr., was very interested in coming to Petersburg for our event, it was the talk of the town. Everyone was excited that Dr. King was coming to Petersburg! Therefore on **March 28, 1962**, First Baptist Church hosted the event: **Eastern Virginia Mass Meeting** (Copy of program is in the Appendix).

First Baptist Church was overflowing with people as we met, with many persons standing outside, just to be in the proximity of greatness. There were at least 1500 people crowded inside and to all of them it symbolized that Petersburg was an actual player in the Civil Rights Movement. In addition, this demonstrated to the Community that black organizations were going to work together to effect change. And though it was a long program, more than three hours in length, we felt energized, not tired at the end. Dr. King gave a marvelous address and I felt like we could accomplish anything that we jointly worked to achieve. Little did I know that my faith in the goodness of man would be tested again and again over the next several years, but that's getting ahead of my story.

In September of 1962, the **Citizenship Schools** were being transferred from the Highlander Folk School in Monteagle Tennessee to the Dorchester Community Center in Hinesville, Georgia. Dr. King wanted all the Staff of SCLC to attend the workshops, if possible, so at this time I was able to attend. I arrived a day early and was greeted by **Mrs. Septima Clark**.

Mrs. Clark began her long career in the South Carolina School system in 1916,when she was 18, at a salary of $35.00/month. She endured the indignity of knowing her white counterparts were being paid $50.00 more per month because she was more concerned about the children of Gullah heritage than the money. However when her name appeared on the rolls of the NAACP in 1956, the school board fired her. Yet, she did not give up. She began working with the Highlander Folk School but when that closed, she joined the staff of the Dorchester Community Center, sponsored by SCLC.

Now as head of our Citizenship School, she was preparing the Community for freedom. As a SCLC staff member, I was there to experience what the students would learn when they arrived.

She asked me to accompany her to the bus station to meet and greet some of the new persons coming for the training. When we arrived, I noticed that all the black people, after purchasing tickets, had to go back outside and await the bus. I went inside to enquire when the bus was due to arrive and was told to wait outside. Well, I was not purchasing a ticket, so Mrs. Clark and I sat down. We were told that we could not sit inside and would have to leave. We remained seated! The police came and told us we had to move outside. When we did not move, he said to me, "Boy, what's your name?" I wouldn't answer. He said again, "Boy, I asked you your name!" I did not answer. He unbuttoned his gun and said, "You are going to answer me!" I still did not speak because I am not a boy. He then told me I was under arrest. As he was putting me into the patrol car, I heard Mrs. Clark, ," Ok, if you are going to arrest him, you'll also have to arrest me because I was with him, sitting in these seats that only white people are permitted to sit!" He really didn't want to arrest her and said, "Lady, I see your name tag and you seem to be a nice lady." I told her to please stay and wait for the students. She agreed but added, "Herbert, if you are not back by this evening, we are coming to get you with bail." We didn't know when the Police station would close or if any bail bondsmen were nearby. In those small towns, you could get arrested and then all of the support systems would close before it was dark. This was the case this time and they wound up keeping me overnight.

Mrs. Clark came the next morning with the bail money and was visibly angry because she had not asked the policeman when they close down for the evening or when the bondsmen would close their offices. Yet when the workshops were over, I went home and never heard anymore about the arrest but with an appreciation for the literacy program.

This experiment in Basic Adult Education, better known as the Citizenship School, became the backbone of the movement. In one week of intense training, adults were given basic literacy skills and an understanding of politics. They came from Virginia, North Carolina, South Carolina and several counties in Georgia and Alabama. Sometimes there were more than 100 persons attending the workshops ranging in age from 13 or 14 to persons over the age of 50! Some had never attended a school in their life and this introduction was life changing because it involved holistic learning.

Not only were voter registration forms introduced to them so that they could become comfortable with the forms, they were also afforded the opportunity to reinforce the learning experience via role-playing. This visual tool was invaluable in aiding the participants and giving them a sense of what they would face. One of the roles I sometimes played was that of a registrar to demonstrate different tactics used to deny the registration. However **Dorothy Cotton, Victoria Gray Adams**, and Mrs. Clark were the teachers and did an exceptional job of instilling pride and hope in the participants. I remember that several of the older students cried when they receive their certificates because this was the first time any of them had received written recognition of any sort.

Yet they had to return home and share what they had learned with their neighbors and were therefore challenged to keep growing. In a little over two years, more than 1,000 persons were trained at the Teacher's Workshops, more than 10,000 students attended their classes, and together, they registered almost 28,000 new voters! What a testimony to the power of people working together for a common cause and to the new found courage to change the systemic oppression existing in America.

I must step back and begin to weave into the story someone especially important to me that you really need to meet. She is the love of my life: **Maxcine Thelma Bullock.**

In the spring of 1963 I was a member of First Baptist Church and very active with the choir and the Young Adult Christian Organization (YACO). Although I had seen Maxcine at the church, I did not know her nor had I ever spoken to her until providence stepped in. There were only two men in the organization and the president, Ms. Mary Wyche, asked me to present some flowers to her. That evening, she looked radiantly beautiful with her hair in a French twist, while wearing a stunning green dress. I was hooked! As I presented the flowers to her, I leaned over close to her ear and whispered "And what are you doing later on tonight?" Her reply was, "None of your business!" Man, I didn't get to first base with her, but she had my 'nose wide open'.

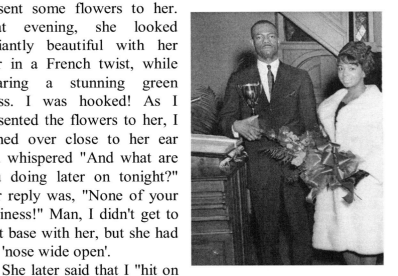

She later said that I "hit on her in the church." And if I remember correctly, my reply was, "You hit where you can when you see someone worthy." She finally agreed to go out with me, on a double date. **James Moses Ballard** was taking a young lady to the Market Inn in Richmond for his birthday and Maxcine agreed to go out with me. I was ecstatic!

When we came back to Petersburg, I invited her to my apartment at 432 Harrison Street for a late night dinner. I was a fair cook and served her fried chicken, greens, potato salad, and rolls; she ate it all! I was about to go to Danville, and though I would be gone for a while, I wanted to assure her that something was happening between us and that I did not want it to end. I told her that I'd be coming back and forth and that I'd call her often. She was different from most of the women I knew and within me, I kept telling myself, "Don't let this woman get away."

We continued to grow closer and I trusted her completely. I even sent her money while I was in Danville to pay my bills and she always took care of things. Once while I was in town, and although our knees were knocking, we spoke briefly with our Pastor, Dr. Milton Reid, about getting married in the Chapel. He told us to get back with him when he returned from a trip to the Holy Land and we could work it out.

In June, Rev. Walker told me it was necessary to get down to **Danville**, **VA** and I was on the highway because Danville was becoming a hot spot and initially, we called it "Little Birmingham." You see the Police and the Fire Departments were bullying people, attempting to intimidate them and going so far, as had occurred in Birmingham, as beating peaceful demonstrators and hosing them down with their water hoses.

"Mrs. Gloria Campbell, the wife of the Reverend Lawrence Campbell, gave this story: When we arrived in this alley between the City Hall and the jail I was on the second row. We sang, 'Jesus keep Me Near the Cross' and after we had gotten in this alley a long line of police formed between the City Hall and the jail. At this point the Reverend McGhee said, 'Let us now bow our heads and pray. He prayed aloud and alone. At this point I saw police come to Bob Zellner and smash his camera and arrest him. Then I saw police go to Reverend McGhee and arrest him while he was praying. Our group was silent. At this time I heard a voice saying, I am tired of you people! I have told you to stay away! Let them have it!' Then I heard laughter.

At this time I saw a fire truck pull up the street about fifty feet and I saw the fire hoses being unwound out in the street. It was a horrible moment to wait for the water to hit us. All of a sudden a great force of water hit me from my back and I was thrown to the pavement with my dress over my head. As I tried to get up I was beaten on my back by a policeman.

We saw policemen standing all around us with long nightsticks. They looked as if they had never been used before.

I saw bodies washed under parked cars just as trash runs down a street after a hard rain.

I heard horrible sounds. Screams like people were being burned up in a fire, the sounds were. As I tried to get up I was beaten in my back. "[2]

My immediate task was to demonstrate that the local government could not intimidate us; and to that end, conduct a massive voter registration drive. To my disappointment the local NAACP Chapter was opposed to the registration drive. For some reason, they wanted to wait until June of 1964. Well, we sensed the mood of the black Community was not one of waiting and we went ahead and began canvassing the black Community to register voters and determine which establishments we would target for picketing.

We would get to our small office early in the morning and begin to pan out over the city to organize and encourage both demonstrators and potential demonstrators. Because of the negative press the city had received, the police and fire departments did not resort to their initial tactics of brutality against its citizens. However, we had to maintain the pressure on the business community because they were not willingly opening the doors of opportunity. Therefore **Bishop Lawrence**

[2] Holt, Len. *An Act of Conscience* (Boston: Beacon Press, 1965, p. 23-24)

Campbell (C.O.G.I.C.), **Rev. Doral Thomas,** Pastor of the largest black church in the city, **Rev. A. I. Dunlop**, a Methodist Minister, and **Rev. L. W. Chase**, Pastor of High Street Baptist worked with me tirelessly to recruit and train the demonstrators and to marshal them to Mass Meetings. Dr. King came to several of our meetings but this was the summer of 1963 and Birmingham was being given a higher priority because of the magnitude of the violence going on there.

We held Mass Meetings almost on a nightly basis to disseminate accurate information, plan our strategies, and solicit assistance from the Community to help us bail out the demonstrators. The beauticians of the city led the way with their generosity of money and food for the marchers and the canvassers. Those sisters would prepare food and close their shops to bring it to wherever we were picketing that day. I hope God continues to bless them wherever they are because we owe them a word of thanks for their courage. **First State Bank**, a local black owned bank, loaned us bail money at no interest and this was appreciated and noted by the local townspeople.

On another level, there were two times I saw Dr. King cry and one of them was that summer. As the number of high school students arrested continued to grow in Birmingham and Danville, he made a personal appeal to the fraternities and sororities to come to the aide of students by bailing them out of jail in the two cities. Not one fraternity or sorority responded! Dr. King cried and said to us, "Well, I guess they (the fraternities and sororities) have outlived their relevancy." He was particularly crushed that his 'brothers', the Alpha's had refused to assist him in this time of need. (It's ironic that now, many years after his death; this same fraternity is spearheading a drive to construct a monument in his honor in Washington, D.C.). So without the local people stepping up, we would not have made it.

In a scene reminiscent of the Wild West, when we arrived at the Circuit Court, the Circuit Judge was openly wearing a pistol.

We are not certain why he felt justified in doing so, but can you imagine the intimidation factor this could cause? Well, we would not be intimidated and shortly thereafter, that practice was stopped. The Voter Registrar's office was operating on a "floating schedule' intended to frustrate us, but we would not be frustrated. The office hours were posted on the door but when we arrived with new registrants, they would close for lunch! If we arrived early in the morning, they would take an early lunch; if we came after 2:00 p.m., they'd close at that point. Further, we knew the FBI was in attendance at our meetings and were tipping off the police because every time we left the meeting and marched, the police officers would be waiting for us, regardless of which route we took. To that end Danville served as the training and testing ground for all of us as we recruited and challenged the people to go to the nation's capitol for the March on Washington.

With our coalition of volunteers, we were able to register thousands of new voters and the NAACP's opposition to the drive did not matter. In a culminating event, we gathered on the eve of the March on Washington and held a prayer vigil at High Street Church and then proceeded to march downtown. Young and old, men and children, walked hand-in-hand, singing and dreaming of freedom and of going to D.C. in the morning. I vividly recall Mr. Pinchback, who had to be at least 80 years old, walking and singing to the top of his voice while encouraging bystanders to join in. There were other elderly persons within the crowd as well, but this man epitomized the spirit of hope that was alive in Danville that night. Most of the residents were united in their opposition to Jim Crow practices and understood the trip to Washington as a political statement of immense importance.

"Herbert Coulton, SCLC Virginia voter-registration expert, got his machinery rolling after several weeks of training volunteer help and canvassing the Negro communities. On his first day set for beginning the actual registration, July 8, fifty-six persons were registered, a record for Danville's voter registration office."[3]

However, on the way downtown, police officers, warned by the FBI of our intentions and following the orders of their superiors, blocked our path and arrested more than 100 of us. Things could have gotten out of hand then, but cooler heads prevailed on both sides and no physical harm was done to any of us. By then we had demonstrated to the City officials that we were followers of a non-violence philosophy and that we were not easily deterred. In addition, we had won the favor of others who were vigilant in watching over us. Ironically I was included in the number of persons arrested and did not get to the March on Washington.

On one level, that's comical because I weighed all of 152 pounds, and was accused of "obstructing the sidewalk." yet, by arresting all of us, the jailers put themselves in a predicament: they were compelled to feed us. After working so hard to get the people involved and willing to participate in the nation wide march, I would not be going. So rather than accept bail, I, along with many others, decided that we would continue their discomfort at least for a while. Still our efforts had lit a fire under many folks and several busloads left Danville, bound for Washington early on the morning of August 28, 1963.

For the next two weeks, I traveled back and forth between Danville, Suffolk, Norfolk, Waverly, Lynchburg, Richmond, and Petersburg. On Friday, **September 13, 1963**, Maxcine ("Max") came to Danville to pick me up because I still did not own a car. My friend Roosevelt Cunningham needed a ride to Richmond and so she agreed to give him a lift. He had to stop by his church, 3rd Street Bethel AME Zion, and since I had always wanted to see the sanctuary, I went inside with him.

---

[3] Ibid, page 204.

Then he said, "Since your Pastor is in the Holy Land and my Pastor is inside, I'm sure he'll marry you." I looked at "Max" and said, "Oh, what the hell!" On that rainy afternoon, Rev. E. William Judge married us! Max did not have on a gown, I needed a shave, but we were just as married as anyone else. She had paid for the license because I didn't have any change and refuses to this day to accept the money back. Instead, she lovingly says, "I own you."

As I look back, she's been an excellent wife, a good friend, and an outstanding mother. I don't think I did badly for a guy who thought he'd forever be a bachelor! My career in the Civil Rights Movement was made smoother because of her unwavering devotion and supportive attitude. When I underwent open-heart surgery, in addition to her other duties, she became my fulltime nurse. Then when she endured a heart attack, I attempted to return the same devotion and care. Unfortunately, I was not up to the task since I was in the midst of recovery myself, but I am eternally grateful to the many friends who stepped in to provide the care she needed. Max, you're still the love of my life and I am so glad that I didn't let you get away!

We didn't have time for a honeymoon because I had to go back to Danville. "Movement wives" have to be as flexible as military wives because we're in one location today, and another tomorrow.

In January 1964, Dr. King promoted me to the position, **Director of Affiliates. Rev. C. T. Vivian** had just resigned and now the responsibility of servicing the 432 Affiliate Chapters fell on my shoulders. This was a National Staff position and I was expected to live in Atlanta, where the home office was located. What was I to do?

Max and I pondered this new assignment and although it was a dream job, there were other considerations to weigh. We still lived in our old apartment and were seeking to purchase our first home. She was pregnant and our entire personal support system was here, in Petersburg! In the final analysis however, Max really did not want to move to Georgia. In her mind, the job would keep me on the road constantly, we had affiliates in 37 states, and this probably meant that she would see even less of me. So we decided that I would eventually go to Atlanta, she would stay here (with her job and our forth coming child), and that I would commute home regularly.

But before I could make the decision, I was called to **Wilmington, NC** by a request from **Golden Frinks**, Field Secretary for North Carolina. This is 1964 and the Klan is active in the area intimidating many people and as a result, tensions were high. Golden told me to come to a small church, **Brown's Chapel** just outside the city limits. There would be a white house next to the Chapel and this would help with the identification, to ensure I was at the proper location. Max was driving; we only had one car, and my friend **Milton West** was along to help her drive back. I am accustomed to arriving at places early, and since it was a dark, gloomy night I took out a match to attempt to read the sign. Max was waiting to make certain we were at the right place before leaving and as I was about to strike the match, the clouds rolled away and a bright moon revealed the name of the church, Brown's Chapel. I went to the house next door, the white house, and the people inside told me, "We're glad you did not strike that match because we had a shotgun pointed at you! Two Klansmen attempted to burn the Chapel last night and we were waiting to see if they had come back. If Golden had told us you were coming, we would have left the porch light on so that you could see." I cannot be sure if my knees began to shake or what, but that was one scary moment. I thank God for watching over me and for allowing the brightness of the moon's glow to reveal who I was!

Let me detour for a brief moment and share a little story with you. While we were dating, Max had asked me how old I was and I didn’t exactly tell her the truth. She was 24 so I held back a year and told her that I was 28, because I didn't want her to know that I was five years older. Well, after our marriage, she still thought I was 28 and when she found out that I had never had a birthday party, Max began to plan one. We were living in the Normandy Apartments on Harrison Street and had moved downstairs where Doris Shepperson Fuller and her husband, Arthur, had moved from. She asked me whom I wanted to invite because she was sending out invitations. I didn't see the need because I could call the few people I wanted to share the occasion with.

My old friend Floyd Henderson was the first to arrive while Max was putting on the final touches. Floyd looked at the candles on the cake, counted them, and said to Maxcine, "I think you left one candle off the cake." I tried to hunch him to tell him, "Just shut up!" but it was too late. Floyd repeated himself, this time a little louder, and Max said, "I know how old my husband is!" "I know how old he is too," Floyd said, "He's four months older than I am." She looked at me and said, with those lovely eyes searching me, "Herbert, is Floyd telling the truth?" All I could say was, "Yes!" I wanted to correct what I had said to her earlier but I didn't. At that moment, all I really wanted to do was take Floyd's head off, but later I thanked him. I had been living a "small" lie, but it came back to bite me. I recall thinking at that moment something like, "truth crushed to the earth shall rise again." I know I am not the first, or the only, man to lie to his wife but I surely did seem small at that moment. Maxcine, I thank you for giving me my first birthday party and even more for forgiving me.

In late fall, as Christmas was approaching, we received an invitation to spend some of the Christmas holidays in Atlanta. We assumed that Dr. King was behind this invitation and that the intent was to convince Max that Atlanta was a good place to be. So along with the roundtrip tickets for the two of us and money for Christmas shopping, there was a personal invitation to stay at the home of **Attorney Randolph Blackwell**, Program Director.

Upon our arrival at the Blackwell's, **Andrew Young** and **Dorothy Cotton** just happened by for lunch and the "wining and dining" of Max was underway. Andy was a Special Assistant to Dr. King at the time and Dorothy, whom we knew from Petersburg, was with the Citizenship Education Program. We really enjoyed ourselves. Besides lunch and the quality time spent getting to know Max, they took us out to see Atlanta and allotted time for Max to shop! And although I could tell that she was very impressed with the people she met, I could not tell if they had really pierced her resolve to remain in Petersburg. So on the plane ride home, I asked her, "Baby, how did you like Atlanta?" When she replied, "I really like the shopping," I knew she had not changed her mind.

Atlanta, in 1964, was similar to other cities at the time, finding it difficult to adjust to the pressures of change. Attorney Blackwell, our host while we were in Atlanta, lived in a very nice section of town on Harland Road, but it was reserved for whites only! In a twist of irony, whites were picketing the area at the time because they did not want open housing in the area. This was not lost on Max and although she never spoke of it, I am certain it factored in her decision not to move to Atlanta.

Plymouth, NC was a small town, gripped by history and unable to move forward, without some assistance. It was the spring of 1965 and Golden Frinks had arranged for me to speak at a Mass Meeting as they geared up to launch a voter registration drive. After the Mass Meeting, our plan was to have a night march to the registrar's office and end the event with prayer. So we marched to the registrar's office, formed a circle and knelt down to pray. As we rose from prayer, we became aware of the KKK, in their regalia, surrounding us.

Golden saw members of the Plymouth police department standing by and asked, "What's the problem officer?" They wanted to know if we had a permit. I said, "No, do we need one?" The officer said, "If you don't stop this demonstration right now, we're going to arrest you!" There were at least 100 people, young and old, who also might be arrested and we wanted to avoid that if possible. As it turned out, they only wanted to arrest the two of us anyway because we were viewed as "trouble makers."

As we were being arrested, we asked one of the local ministers, **Rev. Fred Knox**, if he would lead the people back to the church. When we arrived at the station, they began to process our arrest when an alarm came over their radios. Trouble had broken out.

The Klan with about 125-150 people, had stood around while we were being arrested but when the officers led us away, they became openly hostile. If we were wondering, in the face of open hostility, would our marchers maintain their posture of non-violence, we found out. The Klan began throwing bricks and rocks and immediately one young lady was struck on the head. This in itself was normally not enough to break down a peaceful demonstration, but perhaps the age of the young lady, the language being used to accost us, and the fact of being surrounded caused men to believe their lives were in danger. At any rate, perhaps one too many "Niggers this or nigger that," and a full-scale fight had broken out.

It was then that Golden and I were asked if we would go back to "get our people calmed down." They were willing to release us and would depend on Golden, whom they knew, to come back to the jail when things calmed down. They even threatened to swear out warrants for our arrest if we did not return!

In trying to restore order, we were confronted by the extensive wounds our people had received and the fact that the police was not helping. We wound up calling the State

Police and pressing charges against the local police department through our attorneys affiliated with SCLC. The case did not come to court nor did Golden and I return to be arrested! I have always wondered if the reason we were arrested was so that they would have had a free hand beating the demonstrators. I'll never know but leaving Plymouth I had a deeper respect for Dr. King and the philosophy of non-violence.

In another of the series of events leading up to the passage of the **Voting Rights Act of 1965**, every staff member was asked to campaign in **Alabama**, where 81 candidates were running for office and Dr. king believed that some of them could win. I chose **Bullock County** because that's my wife's maiden name. When I arrived there, I called her and said, "Baby, do you know where I am?" When I told her Bullock County, we both laughed because neither of us had ever heard of the place but thought it was ironic that I was in a place named Bullock, Alabama.

Yet there were four capable, intelligent Black men running for seats on the Board of Supervisor. With four seats vacant and with men whom we believed the Black community could and would support, we felt we had history in our hands. Although many persons were voting for the first time and would not be familiar with voting machines, we were confident.

Since the Voting Committee was planning to hold information sessions in the churches, the local powers were planning a strategy of intimidation. They began calling in the local pastors and advising them not to open their doors. Many of the pastors were justifiably afraid. Their threat was twofold: first, they were really part-time pastors and most had other fulltime jobs, where they could be terminated on the spot! Secondly, if the threat of losing one's source of income was not sufficient to sway a fellow, then the ultimate threat was to bomb the church! Do not forget Birmingham!

As an alternative I suggested that we use the Funeral Homes! It's amazing the opposition this idea received. My argument was that since none of them buried whites, business would not be threatened. They were skeptical because of the stigma attached to funeral homes and because they knew that if they ever needed a loan, since there were no black banks or bankers in Bullock they would require loans from the same white leaders who were trying to intimidate them. Eventually, we met at a funeral home.

Next, as we began going door-to-door with flyers, another residual fear became apparent: many of the local people were afraid to be seen going door-to-door with "out-of-towners." Therefore we had to go alone. We organized committees to provide transportation and food for the workers, telephone callers to encourage voter turnout, others to watch the polling places for irregularities, and successfully showed hundreds how to operate the voting machines. We were prepared and confident of a large turnout!

However, the turnout was extremely low. We discovered that most of the black men worked at menial jobs and their bosses conveniently decided to load them up in large trucks and take them to Florida to pick fruit. Most of the white women were allowed to vote twice: once for themselves and once for their maids. The election officials knew of the practice and allowed it to continue.

We were outraged and began an impromptu demonstration to protest this mockery of liberty. We decided to put caution aside and go directly to the white community and share our disappointment and maybe, just maybe, some might see the injustice of this and align with us, if even secretly. However as we entered the white area, this idea was squashed as the people began to laugh and berate us. Then someone called the police and all of us were arrested for demonstrating without a permit. We knew we didn't have a permit and did not care if they arrested us, this was wrong. Therefore, with all of the resources we poured into Alabama, all we had to show for it the day after election was Sheriff -elect Andison out of Tuskegee.

In 1966, among other places, I visited South Carolina and Mississippi. In South Carolina, in a town called **Mandlin**, I was asked to assist in the voter registration activities. There had never been a successful registration drive in the area and because of my success in other places, I was asked to see what I could do. As I went around town, fear was present in the faces of all I met and I noticed that I was being followed! My personal preference for meetings was always the church, but many locals didn't feel comfortable gathering in groups at isolated churches or even in those located within town limits for that matter. They preferred to meet in homes, which was counter-productive because the homes were too small to accommodate many people. But since they were comfortable with the concept, I thought of the idea as their safety net and went forth.

As one of the "out-of-towners," I was not openly accepted, and so I asked the local Masonic lodge to endorse our door-to-door efforts to add local credibility to our effort. The brothers said no! They were comfortable doing nothing or they were afraid to confront the power structure. Either way, I had a job to do, so we recruited young adults to go door-to-door.

In one of the great ironies of the movement, many of the houses we approached had newly erected "no trespassing" signs in the yards. This was the Black community, occupied entirely by people who looked like us and they were afraid. So, in every instance, I instructed the workers to proceed to the door and ask if the occupants were registered to vote. At one home, the police were waiting for us and threatened to arrest us if we did not move on. At that moment, in my mind, I felt we were bordering on civil disobedience and wondered if getting arrested would be the spark to wake the Community up. We were arrested, but the residents would not press charges against us! Fear had been defeated and many registered to vote.

Then later in the year, I was dispatched to **Jackson, Mississippi** to inspect the King Edward Hotel and, if possible, to reserve a block of rooms for the staff. Jackson had been selected to serve as the host city for our Convention and the King Edward would be our headquarters while there. In those days, flights from Atlanta to other cities in the Deep South were plentiful and were often serviced by small planes with approximately 32 seats, 16 on each side of the aisle.

As I entered the plane, I noticed that that I was the only black person on the flight and that there was only one vacant seat. There was an elderly white woman sitting in the aisle seat and I needed to get past her to take the window seat. I said to her, "Excuse me, may I get through to my seat?" She did not move nor did she act like she had heard me. So I went back up front to see the stewardess to tell her what was going on. The stewardess approached this lady and informed her, "Madam, you will have to move in order for this man to get to his seat." The elderly lady shouted for all to hear, "All my life I have never sat by a Nigger." Eventually, she moved so that I could get to my seat but later a strange thing occurred.

When we took off, the weather was calm but you could see some clouds on the horizon. Shortly thereafter, the plane began to experience heavy turbulence, as it appeared that we were in the midst of a terrible storm. After the plane hit an air pocket and experienced a sudden drop, this lady grabbed my hand, squeezed it, and said, "Mister. Please forgive me for what I said to you earlier, I didn't mean it." She thought she was about to die and did not want that statement on her conscience. I accepted her apology because the Lord still moves in mysterious ways. Even more amazing was the treatment I received in Jackson!

It seems the FBI had contacted the hotel and wanted to make certain we were served. In fact, they insisted so that the rooms could be wired for sound recordings! Therefore the hotel was most accommodating and over priced! Such was the case in most of the places we stayed-the rates were raised because we were black and the rooms were bugged because Dr. King was to stay there.

Later that summer, **1966**, I was working in Virginia doing voter-registering campaigns and while in the Waverly area, I heard of a section called the Wye. This is a small area in Sussex County in what I call "no man's alley." Here there is a distinct and graphic discrepancy between the services offered to the two Communities. One had sidewalks, and indoor plumbing; while the other had outhouses and dirt paths. It's in the heart of a section dominated by the timber companies and most of the work is associated with the lumber mills. Needless to say, most of the families lived in housing without electricity and plumbing for indoor toilets or hot water. Yet the most disheartening situation I ever encountered was the woman with 27 children.

This lady, Mrs. Turner, was 40 years old and had been pregnant every year since she was 13 years old. She helped us to see that we needed to do more than just register the people to vote, they needed life skills.

I told my Pastor, **Rev. Clyde Johnson**, about what we had discovered and he immediately wanted to tour this area to see what First Baptist could offer. The following Sunday Rev. Johnson addressed the congregation and many were astounded and shocked. When the news media became aware of the plight of this area, and especially this family, they gave a full and fair perspective on things. **Dr. Joyce Busch,** a Petersburg physician, called to say she could not go down to Waverly but if we could get the children to her office, she would examine them at no cost. This began a rude awakening for me, and many others, about the effects of malnutrition on children.

Deacon **James Robinson** agreed to take 'Hope', our church bus, down to Waverly to secure the Turner children and take them to Dr. Busch's office. The young people from SCLC would travel down to help clean houses and Rev. Johnson and I were busy cutting hair, although neither of us had a license. On a daily basis **The *Nolde Brothers Bakery*** gave us at least a box of bread and then we would stop at **Hick's Grocery**, a black owned store in Waverly, to purchase peanut butter, strawberry and grape preserves, and bologna to feed the Turner children.

School was out for the summer so we were able to get teachers from Petersburg and Sussex County to come down and set up impromptu classrooms. It was at this time that we found out the Turner children had never been to school! We recruited students from Peabody High School and Virginia State College to help us clean and paint the interior and exterior of homes. Rev Johnson, after inspecting the beds, was busy burning the mattresses because they were infected with lice! We reported the horrible conditions of poverty and some were offended that we were exposing the underside of the richest nation in the world.

The Progress Index newspaper carried the story and caring people stepped forth and did what they could to ease some of the misery, not just of the Turner family, but also for other families living in this area. At the forefront in the giving of money for this effort were **Bland** and **Peace Funeral Homes**. Among the churches stepping up to assist us we must list First Baptist of Petersburg and First Baptist of Waverly at the top of the list. In addition to donating linen and bedding for the families, **J. C. Penney** also allowed a 'Community donation box' so that members of the Community could also assist.

While this was an outstanding response from the private sector, we also wanted a positive political response. With that in mind, we invited the Virginia legislature to come and see for themselves the horrible living conditions. **Governor Mills Godwin, Jr.**, had publicly stated, *"I know of no place in Virginia where poverty exists as bad as what is being reported"* and we were calling his hand on this matter. So we cleared off a vacant lot, cut the grass, and set up chairs from the two churches and the funeral homes for a public assembly meeting. We placed the names of every state senator and delegate from the Commonwealth on one of the chairs. We sent invitations to their Richmond addresses and posted an advertisement in the newspaper. However, only **Henry Howell**, famous for his slogan, *"Keep the big boys honest,"* cared enough or was curious enough to come. In spite of the poor response of our own representatives, our actions did reverberate around the nation's capitol and at least one significant person was watching with more than casual interest.

The person paying close attention was **U.S. Senator Robert Kennedy (D-NY),** the former President's brother. The Senator invited **Nathaniel Hawthorne** of Lunenburg County and me to Washington D.C. to testify about the conditions we witnessed personally, and to detail what we were attempting to do to combat poverty. He was so engrossed in what was happening that a private plane was dispatched to transport us!

As the Christmas season approached, Rev. Johnson suggested to **John Long** (a member of Bethany Baptist and an employee at Ft. Lee), along with some other adults, to spearhead a drive to make Christmas special for this family in the Wye. When I arrived home, I shared with Maxcine that whatever money I would have spent on her for Christmas would be used to purchase gifts for some of the people living in the Wye. We were making a small difference and it felt good. I don't know if that section of Sussex County even exists today, but I do know that the people were given a seed of hope and they nourished it. Many of the young people participated in **Job Corp** and went on to lead productive lives. Needled to say, Governor Godwin was now informed of impoverished conditions in Virginia.

"I had just graduated from North Carolina A &T in the spring and returned home. It was not uncommon then for girls to go off to college and then return to Petersburg. Some of the women I knew, all college grads, formed a club called

"Laisatwa" (The Ladies) and we were into what is now called community outreach. When we heard about what was being disclosed about the Wye, we had to put on our Florence Nightingale hats and do our best. After Jesse Jackson had us marching back and forth down at A&T (North Carolina) this just seemed natural.

But the squalor we found in the Wye was unbelievable. But we rolled up our sleeves and did what we could. We cleaned those girls and took them clothes, had their hair done, and even took them shopping. But they had learned some habits that we could not undo. You know, living in Petersburg, we were all poor, but we had never seen conditions like this." **Florence Jones Clark** is presently an Adjunct Professor, at VSU. She is a former member of the State Board of Nursing and a former volunteer in the Movement.

As a part of our campaign to win our right to vote Dr. King visited **Suffolk, VA** often in the early sixties, especially between1962-65. There were festering problems within the Peanut Industry and with Obici Hospital. During these annual visits, he would visit Suffolk Ball Park for a mass meeting and sometimes engage us in softball at one of the nearby fields. On this particular visit however, the local leadership wanted a night march. Of course they wanted Dr. King to lead it but also had secured Cleveland Robinson from a national union, Rev. Curtis Harris, and myself. Mr. Robinson was legally blind so Rev. Harris and I sandwiched him as we marched. As evening became night, a series of shots rang out! Uncertain of where the shots were coming from, our strategy was to return to the office of the Peanut Company. **Mr. Lock Parker**, a local Black Union leader, informed us that in spite of the number of shots, only a minor wound had occurred- one young man had a leg wound. A sick feeling came over me as if a premonition of pending disaster loomed large in my mind. All of us knew the danger associated with what we were attempting and death was a constant companion. And at that moment, when the shots were fired, I just knew it was the end…for me. Yet, God had other plans for me.

Herbert, Jr.: "Unto us a son ..."

Meanwhile, during the summer of 1964, I had moved to Atlanta to be closer to the work. I moved initially into a rooming house of Mrs. Sheets but this proved uncomfortable. I relocated to the William Holmes Borders Apartments but that also did not work out. Finally, I settled in with **Mrs. Juanita Hill,** an employee of Citizen's bank in Atlanta. From this arrangement I tried to commute home at least twice per month. Max was at home about to deliver our first born and the thought of fatherhood was pressing.

I had never really thought about having a child until Max told me she was pregnant. My two brothers had girls (Richard and Emma one daughter, Bettye; Marvin and Annie had three girls: Brigette, Muriel, and Francoise). My sister had a son, Gregory, but he was not a Coulton. I felt in order to keep the name alive, I needed a son, and therefore I began praying for a son.

Sometimes when Max would talk to her friends, I would hear her say, "When it comes," and that word would bother me immensely. So I began interrupting her and saying, "When he comes." I think she would have been happy with a healthy baby, but I wanted a son. We even began to buy 'blue' in the fifth month. At that time, you did not find out the sex until the arrival, but somehow I knew. I remember when Max was ready to go to the hospital, we chose St. Phillip's in Richmond. We felt the facilities were better than what was available for blacks at Petersburg General Hospital.

When the time arrived**, Joe and Gloria Cooper**, our friends from Shore St., took us to Richmond. I came back home and didn't sleep at all that night. I decided to paint the apartment so that when Max and the baby came home, they would come to a spruced up place. We lived in the Normandy Apartments, owned by one of my former teachers, Mrs. Josephine Walker Jones. Knowing that Maxcine was expecting, she said to me, "Herb, don't pay me for this month. You buy that baby some milk." It's one thing to say you care about your tenants but her actions demonstrated her care.

So after painting all night-the stairway and three rooms, I laid down for an hour or two to rest. At about 7:30 that morning I decided to call the hospital. When the receptionist came on the line, I asked had my son been born? She asked my name and after a ten-minute wait she came back with these words, "Yes, your son has been born"! I asked, "Are you sure?" She said, "Yes, I'm sure. He was born at 7:07 and weighed 7lbs.2oz ." I was filled with joy! Although Max had several names if it was a girl, I had only one name in mind, Herbert Vanlot Coulton, Jr.

(In this family photo, Herbert, Jr. is quietly being restrained by our hands; our hidden hands are actually doing most of the work. 1965)

Even until this day, he does not care for his middle name. He wanted to know the history of the name and all that, but the only answer I had for him was that my daddy put it on me and I was doing it to him. He didn't pass the name on to his son however, choosing Jalen Micah instead.

Jalen Micah Coulton and Grandpa

I was so happy and proud when Max and Herbert, Jr. came home. I wanted to do so many things to put my whole life into this little guy. But I remembered Michael Levine saying, "Having children makes one no more a parent than having a piano makes you a pianist." So as busy as I was, I needed to find some quality time for him.

I remember when Herb, Jr. was at the Day Care at Gillfield Baptist Church and they were having a graduation exercise. I felt compelled to be there and remember saying, "I just have to go to that graduation because this might be the only time he graduates from anywhere." I mean, you never know.

So with that as a backdrop, after coming home to my family, I was on the floor playing with Herbert, Jr. and asked him who I was and he said, "man." Not daddy, but just man, I decided right then I had to make some changes.

That Monday morning, after returning to Atlanta, I went to the Executive Staff meeting and told Dr. King I would have to come home because my son did not know me. He understood because he had children that barely knew him. His only concern was that by returning to Virginia, I not give up on the movement. I assured him that I would continue what I had begun, just not from Atlanta.

Later that year, 1967, at perhaps my last meeting as Director of Affiliates, we met in Louisville, Kentucky and were hosted by Mohammed Ali. The Champ met us at the airport and treated the entire traveling group to lunch, with the exception of one of the ladies traveling with us. She was wearing a dress that revealed her knees and Ali would not dine with a woman who showed her knees. I stayed throughout the session but that was my last official function as Director of Affiliates. After that, I returned to Virginia to continue my work and the work of the movement as Field Secretary for Virginia.

High school and college students knocking on doors, registering persons to vote in Petersburg, VA (Herbert Coulton, 1961)

Poor Peoples Campaign

In early 1968, Dr. King said, "We must have a program centered upon jobs and economic opportunities." He was broadening our sense of the possibilities and causing us to think in terms of finding creative, non-violent actions to address these areas affecting not just African Americans but all the poor people living in America.

Marian Wright Edelman, a knowledgeable and compassionate woman guided us and proved to be a most valuable resource for us, and many others as well involved in raising awareness and providing information and strategies to overcome some of the social ills facing America. Not only had she worked among the poor of Mississippi, but also had spent time in Washington D.C. gleaning knowledge of the available programs already on the law books. To her dismay, many of those who could be helped by the programs were unaware of their existence! When she informed Dr. King of the magnitude of the matter, he was not discouraged but appeared to get angry. But he also realized that this was an opportunity to broaden the movement and transcend the traditional platform of civil rights for Blacks. And he knew that some difficult days lay ahead, trying to convince poor whites that our common positions of poverty made us allies. However never one to accept defeat before the battle was fought, we went confidently ahead.

First, Dr. King had to present the program to the Board of SCLC for their approval. Then divergent strategies were outlined to get the word out and invite others to walk with us. So therefore, in March leaders from other minority groups (Puerto Ricans, Mexicans, American Indians, and whites from Appalachia) were invited to Atlanta to set an agenda for cooperation. This was a major undertaking and the sheer logistics alone were enough to stop the plan before it occurred.

Housing encampments, food, medicinal supplies, water, and toilets had to be provided for an anticipated one million people in Washington, D.C.!

Then the Field Secretaries were alerted to spread the word in their respective areas of our intent for a rally in Washington, D.C. In that regard, **Andy Young** called me to put together a **"People To People"** tour in Virginia. Dr. King wanted to come to Virginia to shake hands, encourage participation, and lend his persona to this phase of planning. His planned itinerary would be Atlanta to Norfolk, then Suffolk, Ivor, Waverly, Hopewell, Petersburg, and culminating in Richmond before returning to Atlanta. Both Dr. King and Andy Young signed off on the itinerary, but it never happened. Instead, Dr. King went to Memphis, Tennessee.

Memphis Tennessee!

In March of 1968, the sanitation workers of Memphis went on strike and invited Dr. King to advocate on their behalf. No, this was not an invitation to receive the keys to the city or to speak to the Board of Education; it was a trip to rub shoulders with garbage workers and lead a demonstration on their behalf. Dr. King was concerned when the first march ended in the violent death of a young man and was determined to lead a peaceful march. This march was planned for April 8.

Andy Young called me to inform me that Dr. King would have to postpone the **People To People Tour** in VA because of Memphis and would get to me after April 8th. Meanwhile, the Mayor of Memphis had obtained a federal injunction against residents marching or demonstrating but Dr. King was determined to lead this particular demonstration.

On Thursday, April 4th, I was invited to come and speak to the African American Club at VSU. The meeting was scheduled for 7:30 p.m. on the 3rd Floor of Foster Hall. I am usually early when I have something to do but this night I was extremely early. I arrived at 6:30 p.m. and was sitting in the lobby listening to the news. I remember that the reporter said that Dr. King had been shot but that he could not confirm his condition. Two minutes later, he announced that Dr. King was dead! I left Foster Hall immediately and went to the state office of SCLC!

Petersburg, like many other cities, was in an uproar. On Friday morning, I received a call from **Elmore Rainey**, principal of Peabody High School, asking me to come speak with the students to help them in their anger and grief. I went immediately. Part of what I shared were some words I had heard from Dr. King: *"If we have a confrontation and I blacken your eye and then you blacken my eye, all that we have proved is that we have the capacity to blacken each other's eyes. The problem still exists."* My final words to them were not to remember Dr. King with acts of violence. I told them that many of the Black churches would hold Memorials Services all over town and they would be welcome at any of the services. Emphatically, I urged them all to calm down and go home because the National Guard was on alert and was being deployed around downtown areas.

Saturday passed with little violence but on Sunday we held a meeting on the Court House steps on Sycamore Street. To an extremely large gathering I shared, as calmly as possible, not only my deep grief but also that Dr. King's funeral was scheduled for Tuesday, April 9th and that I, and a delegation from Petersburg, would be attending.

On Monday, the delegation boarded a flight for Atlanta: **Mrs. Cassie Walker** (owner, Little Lady Beauty Salon), **William N. Bland, Sr., Rev. Clyde Johnson** (my pastor), **Edward B. Farley** (Dinwiddie High School teacher) and myself. After arriving at our hotel, we placed our bags in the rooms and took a cab to Ebenezer Baptist Church. A very orderly, but long line of persons was waiting to get in to view Dr. King's body so we got in line as well. The first person we recognized in the line was **William J. Alexander** of Brunswick County. How had he beaten us there? He told us that he thumbed some and took a bus the remainder of the way. But his determination was represented in the faces and stories of many that day that were determined to see the body of Dr. Martin Luther King, Jr.

And although I was saddened by the occasion, I was somehow gladdened by the turnout and the respect it demonstrated. I need you to know that Dr. King had planned the sermon used on that for the day for the upcoming Sunday service. He had discussed it with his brother, Rev. A.D. King and AD did not change much if any of it. The title of the sermon was, *" Why America May Go To Hell,"* seemed to be playing out on the streets of America that week.

Meanwhile, we arrived back in Petersburg on Wednesday and immediately began to address the violence of our own community. I called **Hermanze Fauntleroy** and we agreed to go into some of the neighborhoods and confront anger head on. Many angry young men had already broken out the windows of the buildings on Harrison Street, from Halifax up towards Bland's Funeral Home. In fact, a rumor was spreading that they planned to bomb Brown & Williamson Tobacco Company. We said to them, "Look, we understand your anger but if you do this, where will your parents work?" Several in the group were children of employees of Brown & Williamson and this made a difference in their thinking! We asked them to call it off, please! We even went with them to phone booths to listen to their calls to ensure that the word got out. Then someone suggested that they burn down a neighborhood! We countered, "Then where would your family and the families of your friends live?" After cursing some and even crying some, they went home. Fortunately God gave us the proper words and body language to reason with these young men or Petersburg could have made the news like Washington, D.C. or Detroit or Los Angeles. In spite of the difficulty of the times, the poor People's Campaign went on as planned...but it was not the same without Dr. King. Many people were still in mourning and chose not to attend. Others came, but did not stay very long sensing that the voice behind the drive was missing.

In the aftermath, many members of the executive staff determined it was time to leave the SCLC. Some had committed to work as long as Dr. King stayed and now felt that their commitment was over! Dr. Wyatt Walker had left earlier but his absence now was very noticeable. While on board, Dr. Walker, an excellent manager and organizer, kept things in National Office and in the Field Offices running smoothly. But now, with Dr. King's death and his absence, many of the things needed for a smooth operation were missing and relationships were becoming frayed.

Yet, there were still good people determined to stay the course and finish the work like Andy Young and Hosea Williams, who stayed until his death. However many persons left to resume their careers or to seek other employment. Although I was now out of the National Office and spotlight of Atlanta, I stayed on in the Virginia State Unit of SCLC until October 1999, serving a total of 41 years.

Chapter 3:
A New Career-Beyond SCLC

"When loving hearts are separated, not the one which is exhaled to heaven, but the survivor, it is which tastes the sting of death." Duchess de Praslin

What does a man do after working with the most dynamic organization, in the most trying times in the life of his country? How do you reconcile the fact that the prophet of non-violence was another victim of the reactionary violence rising in American society? With these and other questions, unanswered and grieving my very soul, I began the search for a new career.

As I searched for work I heard about a company called **Job Skills Training**. **B. J. Roberts**, a progressive person who happened to be white, had formed this company with grants from the federal government and was looking for local people to align themselves with. He had gone to several of the workshops sponsored by the National SCLC convention in Atlanta, was impressed by Andrew Young, and wanted to effect change.

His heritage indicated a mixture with the Native American people and he was sensitive to the plight of disadvantaged groups. And although his father was bigoted toward blacks, he was of another disposition. I found out later that my old friend Hermanze Fauntleroy had given him my name believing that we were both interested in making an impact in the world and could possibly work together. As I investigated his resources, I learned that he had secured a sizable contract with the Seward Luggage Company to allow 100 of its new employees to take the training and I was swayed to come on board.

So in May of 1970, Harold Reid and I began the Petersburg operation. Harold was also white and a former employee of

Seward where he was not only a machine operator and but was exceptionally mechanically inclined. I, on the other hand, was expected to maintain the administrative side of things. What I didn't anticipate was that we would be expanding on lessons learned in the Freedom Schools and intentionally teaching life skills. This was because many of our students came from impoverished families, overlooked by society and left upon the dunghills of life. Poverty has an awesome stench and its tentacles cloud the expectancy of some and leaves others drowning in the sea of despair.

Many of those enrolled in our program were not accustomed to coming to work on time or on a daily basis. We wanted to eliminate all excuses for not being available for training so we paid for a reliable baby sitter as well. At the time, this was a first! In addition, our interactions with company nurses raised the issue of family planning and we offered sessions on birth control to the ladies of childbearing age. We wanted them to assume control of their bodies, to be aware of the availability of birth control measures, and to have planned pregnancies. None of the ladies had health insurance and very few had ever had check ups.

With the men our emphasis was on good work habits and personal responsibility. Not only did we stress punctuality for work but also performance on the job. We showed them the direct correlation between good performance on the operation of the machines and promotions.

Everyone was exposed to lectures and filmstrips on Black history to enhance their pride and to make them aware of the contributions to society made by Black people. And although it was not a portion of the curriculum, I always included voter registration information and encouraged them to be participatory citizens.

Seward Luggage was the largest luggage company in the world at that time. In addition to contracts providing footlockers for West Point Military Academy, the company also did specialty work for the stars of Hollywood. Her most famous client at the time was the actress Elizabeth Taylor. And of course the average wage amounted to about $1.50 per hour and was insufficient to provide for a family.

Meanwhile Brown & Williamson Tobacco Company, a sound firm of the City was hiring and applicants were lining up at the personnel office on Market Street. Company officials from Seward Luggage would ride by these lines and photograph all the persons in line. If any of their workers were spotted in the enlarged photographs, they were fired immediately. How cruel! You are paying $1.50 per hour, yet resented anyone from trying to better his or her life. (Brown & Williamson only advertised entry-level jobs but those paid an average of $5.00 per hour!)

So B.J. and I intervened on behalf of the displaced workers and in most instances were able to persuade Seward to re-instate them. Yet these incidents lit a fire under some of the workers and they went on to better paying jobs and lived very productive lives. Some of the other contracts we were able to secure included Kenleh Furniture in Kenbridge and McKinney, VA and USCO of South Hill, a maker of modular homes. The latter had an order to make more than 2500 houses for the Virgin Islands and several thousand more for Honduras after the hurricanes of 1970. By 1979, most of the federal grants had run their course and it was time for me to move and seek other employment.

Life Insurance Company of VA

I saw an advertisement in the newspapers indicating that Life of Virginia was looking for sales representatives and I applied. At the time there was only one other Black person in the Petersburg office but I was not deterred. I went to the Manager's office for the interview and he asked me did I think I could sell insurance. "I can sell anything," was my comment to him! He replied, "Well at least you are confident!" I was hired on a trial period and was told that when I was ready to take the Life and Health exams, required for the license, to let them know so that he could assist me.

All I needed to know was where in Richmond I needed to go to take the test. I found out, went over and took the test and made 100 on both. When I came back to work I said to him, "I'm ready to seek some clients." He said, "But you have to take the test!" I showed him my grades and all he could say was, "Well Mr. Coulton, you are ready!"

Life Insurance Company of Virginia was a good company. They sold all the supplemental and retirement insurance to the state workers, especially all of the teachers in the state. It was strange that no other insurance company contested their monopoly but I was not going to raise that issue.

However, in spite of the reputation of the product, it was still a 'good ole boy company'. I was there four more years before another black person applied for employment. So I had to pay my dues in more ways than one.

Each year all of the agents in the company were asked to turn in projections for the ensuing year. Most of them gave an amount that considered very modest-less than one million dollars. I always thought that I would sell at least a million dollars.

When I made the Million Dollar Roundtable, I told all of the agents that they should be selling more insurance than I was able to because they had an open door to blacks as well as whites, while I only had an open door to some blacks. No white folks opened their doors to me.

In somewhat disbelief I related this story. My first call was on a black woman who knew that my product was good and that my presentation was excellent. When I finished, the woman said to me, "If you would send a white agent to my house and if he would present the product in the same manner-I will buy it! I don't buy anything from black folks!" Later on she admitted a bias because she had been 'burned' by a black salesman and would never buy anything from black people. I asked her had a white salesman ever disappointed her and she said yes and smiled. To me this said that many of us still think that a white man's ice tea is sweeter and his ice is colder. We have been brain washed into thinking if it is black, then it must be inferior.

Life of Virginia afforded me many opportunities to demonstrate my skills in salesmanship and to compete for bonus trips as a direct result thereof. I won trips to many places: Virginia Beach, Lake Tahoe, the Virgin Islands, and Bermuda to name some of them. However the trip that stands out in my mind was to Bermuda because I was chosen to speak at our convention.

Five of us made the MDRT (Million Dollar Round Table) and each of us was afforded an opportunity to speak on a topic selected by the 'big dogs'. We would have a maximum of twenty minutes and our speech had to be seen by Mr. Sam Turner, President of Virginia Life before we arrived. So I sent a copy of the speech to Mr. Turner.

Although one of the company secretaries had neatly typed the speech, when I arrived in Bermuda I decided I was not going to deliver that speech! Instead I rose early that morning and went out on the hotel balcony and began to write another speech. My wife joined me on the balcony and when she found out what I was doing, she thought I was crazy. I told her that might be true but I was not going to deliver that prescribed speech. In my mind, that which they had was what they wanted to hear but I wanted to do something else. I wanted to tell them what was on my heart and I might not get another chance. You see I wanted to tell them about one of my clients, Marvin Cox.

I sold a policy to Marvin's mother first because it was one she could afford and secondly, because it would provide the coverage she needed for her six children. Marvin was 15 years old and had developed bone marrow cancer which, his doctors believed did not give him long to live. While Marvin appeared to be ok with dieing, his only regret was that he did not have a bicycle and he shared with me that he wanted one desperately. Therefore, I called the radio station and told them my intentions of raising money for this effort.

So along with Debra Powell, a nurse at Petersburg General Hospital and a member of our Sunday School Class, I placed a table in the parking lot of First Baptist Church to offer the Community an opportunity to make this wish come true. With the radio station encouraging donations, the turnout was great. Not only did we receive enough for Marvin's bike, but we were also able to buy presents for the other five children as well. We could have purchased the bicycle ourselves but we wanted to give the Community an opportunity to come to the aid of this family.

Marvin died a few months after and his mother used that policy to provide for his funeral and to secure her future. I will never forget Marvin and felt it was more important to share his story than what Mr. Sam Turner wanted me to talk about. His mother was very appreciative and to this day, she thanks me. You can't go wrong doing what's right!

Chapter 4:
The Church

"...and on this rock I will build my church, and the gates of Hades will not overcome it." (Matthew 16: 18, NIV)

If we live a normal life, we would live some 25, 550 days. Well, God has already allowed me to live beyond that (26,745 and counting) and many of those days have been spent in the church. Even when I was in the military, two of my buddies and I would go to the church wherever we were stationed. I guess the church is all I know!

When we were in Hawaii, it was First Baptist Church in Wahiawa that we attended. There were only four blacks in the congregation and one, Mrs. Mary Brown of Prince George County sang in the choir. Now what are the chances of someone from around the corner from me would be singing in the choir? Well, there she was and although it was not home, but it felt good.

From the base, Wahiawa was about the distance from Petersburg to Ft. Lee. So my friends, Aaron Houston (Louisville, Ky.) and John Prioleau (Augusta, Ga.) and I would walk there every Sunday that we were not on duty. There were no buses on Sunday and we did not have a car, so we walked. During the week, there was maybe a game of football or baseball to occupy our leisure, but Sunday service was our main activity.

Even though I was made to attend church as a youngster, I now attend because I want to. I believe Jesus calls us not only to come to him but also to go for him. During my adult life, I have tried to go for him. But let me tell you how this all began, this church thing and me.

First Baptist of Petersburg

I first came to First Baptist of Petersburg, the oldest African American Baptist Congregation in the United States, in the company of the Chair of the Deacon Board, Bennett R. Powell. Deacon Powell would come to our house by 9:00 a.m. and the Pastor, Rev. W. W. Roberts, would pick us up. I was 13 years old at the time and remember being baptized that fall. That was 60 years ago and I have been there ever since. You see the Lord didn't bring me this far to leave me. I have always loved the passage that says, "So in Christ we who are many form one body, and each member belongs to all the others." (Romans 12:5 NIV).

Therefore I am grateful to First Baptist Church for allowing me the space and the time to grow in grace. She has been a 'movement church' (active in the Civil Rights Movement) and the members have granted me the privilege of keeping them informed. We were not only concerned about civil rights but also human rights and social justice issues. So any time one of these or related issues was stirring, they allowed me, and others to address the matter publicly. All of the pastors, Rev. Milton Reid, Rev. Clyde Johnson, Rev. Robert Jemison, Rev. Dr. Harold Carter, Jr., Rev. Gilbert Campbell, and our present servant, Rev. Dr. Jeremiah Tillman either informed the congregation of important matters or allowed a lay person to do so. And so First Baptist is alive and vibrant today because the Shepherds have kept us abreast of spiritual issues to invigorate our souls and political matters to inspire us to action.

Pastors/Preachers

Now, because of my position as Director of the Affiliates with the Southern Christian Leadership Conference (SCLC), I have been privileged to come in contact with many pastors and preachers over the years. Many have been warriors in the struggle for civil rights and human dignity and I applaud them all. But far too many of those I have personally met were very disappointing. My good friend, the late Dr. William Augustus Jones, Jr. in his book, *God In The Ghetto*, sums it up like this:[4]"The Black Church became the new Africa. It was the extended family restored under the leadership of Jesus Christ, the great High Priest and under the earthly directions of the Black preacher, who was prophet, priest and village chief." But he goes on to say, "The Black preacher unfortunately is often a hindrance to the advancement of the Black cause. Some still are inactive in the struggle because of their failure to see the social implications of the Gospel." [5]

What Bill was declaring matched my observations far too often. It was not uncommon to hear some preachers make comments like: "It's only my task to preach the gospel and win souls for Jesus. The rest (social betterment, progress, etc.) is not my business!" This mindset or theology left many congregations on the outside of the movement. They were merely observers to a great move toward freedom and therefore socially impotent. How often I wanted to grab some of the pastors and physically shake them alert to the prophetic possibilities around them, but I didn't. I realize that fear gripped many of them and still others were co-opted by the power structure!

Another observation that has troubled me is that so many uneducated ministers, some having a questionable bachelor's degree, and most just seminary degrees, being awarded or somehow acquiring doctoral degrees. Perhaps you may think this is petty, but if you need an honorary or bogus degree to validate who you are, I have a problem with that. Perhaps I am sensitive to this because I have known so many men and women

---

[4] Jones, William A. Jr. *God In The Ghetto* (Elgin, Illinois: Progressive Publishing, 1979) p. 122

[5] Ibid, page 123

who have studied for many years and labored many hours to acquire their credentials that this undermines their accomplishments somehow in my mind. But, if some of these folks were not so arrogant to demand that I address them as "Dr..." I would not make an issue of it.

In my activities at First Baptist, I have been a Sunday school teacher, Chairman of the trustees, business manager of the Male Chorus, and a member of the Cathedral Choir. Because of my involvement with church, the Community has asked me to serve on Community Outreach teams and become involved with Campus Ministry at Virginia State University. In fact, under the urging of my good friend Victoria Adams, I served several years as the Chair of the Board of Directors of United Campus Ministry (VSU). It was while serving on that Board that I became familiar with my co-writer, James Daniely. In all, I served the Campus Ministry board for some 12 years before I retired.

Virginia T. Anderson Sunday School Class

But that's getting ahead of the story. I was discharged from the Army in February 1959 and immediately returned to First Baptist Church. My Pastor, Rev. Milton Reid welcomed me with open arms and wanted me to find a place to connect. As I looked around, I saw progress. For example, the pot belly stove that once was housed in the basement had been removed and a central heating unit was in place. The baptismal pool, where I had been baptized, was now relocated in a different area of the building. And most impressive, there were very many young adults worshiping each week.

Then Ms. Dorothy Meade approached me with an idea: form a Young Adult Class. Well, she suggested that I approach Rev. Reid with a proposal and he told me to present it to the Board of Deacons. So I went to the Church's business meeting and proposed that we honor one of our long term members by forming a class in her honor (Virginia T. Anderson). They approved it and designated Beatrice Graves and me as the teachers.

We were young and with a large pool of other young adults, we were able to gather a good number for the class. We were not 'bible teachers' so our class was not the normal Sunday school Class. Every month we planned outings into the Community to observe, ask questions, and determine what we could do to help our Community. If someone told us about a situation, we would look into it and see if we could make a difference.

This may sound unbelievable to some but let me tell you a true story. We were told that there was an elderly member of the Community who lived on Virginia Avenue who needed help. So I took two of the young women, Daphne Abraham and Barbara Bishop, with me to her home to see what was going on. We knocked on her door several times without getting a response and then began to leave. Once we were off the porch, an old lady came to the door and said, "I heard you knocking but I was still praying because I had eaten my last slice of bread last night and was asking God for help." We were touched beyond belief and went inside to see what we could realistically do. Well, she had no food and we knew we'd take care of that; but without being intruders, we wanted to see if we could do a little more. The house needed cleaning so we put on our list of items to purchase: a mop, broom, liquid cleaners, sheets, pillow cases and a spread. We went shopping and returned to her house where we were able to clean it, make the bed, and prepare the meal. She protested a little but we could tell that she really appreciated what we had done.

So when we told the other class members what we had done, they also became excited and wanted to participate in 'good deeds'. The class began to look for opportunities to help their neighbors. If someone needed wood cut or warm clothes, the Virginia T. Anderson Class was willing to help. Thanksgiving was approaching and we wanted to feed as many people as possible. Since we didn't have a lot of money we looked in the Community for partners. **Wyche's Confectionary**

Store offered the can goods at their cost and **Liberty Markets** sold us chickens in bulk. As a result, we were able to provide a complete meal for 25 families. We did the same thing for Christmas!

About this time, Rev. Reid came to me and said, "Brother Coulton, you have shamed me." I said to him, "What have I done?" He said, "Your Sunday school class is giving out food baskets when this should be something your church is actively leading." So he went before the Deacon Board and secured the money to do the Christ-like thing: feed the hungry in the Community.

First Baptist became the front runner in feeding the hungry of Petersburg. Now, we give out approximately 300 total food baskets for Thanksgiving and Christmas. And not just to members of First Baptist, but to any who ask. In addition, we offer meals to the homeless on a daily basis.

The Virginia T. Anderson Class was concerned about the Community. We took the name of a grand ole lady, whom I admired, and began a new movement, if you will. We pooled our resources by taking a special offering each week to begin a food pantry, can goods only at first so that there was "food in my house," as one of the prophets said. As word spread of what we were doing, the membership grew until we maxed out at 64 members. Eventually, the church took responsibility for the food pantry and later added a clothes closet also to attempt to meet the needs of the needy in the Community.

The Virginia T. Anderson Class finally said they wanted to take a trip! The trip was to Washington, D.C. and it was not an enjoyable one. But as our first venture away from Petersburg, it was a learning experience. Since that time, we have taken more than 25 trips and the venue has been varied. Trips to New York, Toronto, Atlanta, Disney World, California, Hawaii, and even over seas to London/Paris have been a part of our itinerary. We have also taken cruises to San Juan, St. Martin, Barbados, St. Thomas, and Alaska. We even sponsored a car raffle and raised enough money for the entire class to travel free to Disney World and still donate $2000.00 to the church.

Yet to some, the crowning achievement of this wonderful class was an annual event, taking young people (middle and high school students) to New York and exposing them to a Broadway play. We would then take in either Rev. Wyatt Walker's or Dr. Bill Jones' worship service on that Sunday to complete the experience.

Many of them had never ventured beyond Petersburg and most had never gone out of Virginia. But to see their eyes beam when seeing the Empire State Building for the first time or to experience a Broadway production was very rewarding. At times, it appeared that a whole new horizon was opening before their very eyes. How do you measure the impact this had on their self esteem to be able to speak intelligently about places that were once only words in a geography textbook?

This has been a wonderful class. We learned from each other and grew together. We are especially proud that our children were welcomed to attend with us. Over time some died, some stayed here, but others moved away and hopefully took the lessons learned with them to other classes and other churches.

But last year (2006) we had a class reunion in July on the 28th and 29th. What a wonderful sight to see so many, who had successful careers as teachers, government workers, health care professionals, or army officers, to come together and celebrate what God was doing with us. Our banquet was on Saturday (28th) and we worshiped together on that Sunday (29th). Some of us had not seen each other in years so it was extremely good fellowship. There might be a better church school somewhere…I just don't know where it is.

That class deepened my faith, by allowing me to put my faith in action. But on another level, I was still a child in the faith. I Corinthians talks about becoming a man and putting away childish things. Well for me, that was getting a full understanding about stewardship of my money. To that end, I listened carefully to what Dr. Wyatt T. Walker had to say. In many of his revivals, he spoke on tithing, giving a tenth of your income to the church. He stated on several occasions, "I know tithing works because God never had a plan that did not work well." That intrigued me because at that point, I was not giving in that manner. Then I ran across *Common Thieves* in which he states," What I gave, I have; what I spent, I had; but what I kept, I lost."[6]

[6] Walker, Wyatt T. *Common Thieves (*New York, M.L.K. Fellows Press, 1986) p.47

Chapter 5:

Majoring in Minors

"Men die, but sorrow never dies;
The crowding years divide in vain,
And the wide world is knit with ties
Of common brotherhood in pain." Susan Coolidge

"O sorrow, wilt thou rule my blood,
But sometimes lovely, like a bride,
And put thy harsher moods aside,
If thou wilt have me wise and good." Tennyson

What I have to say now creates a great sorrow in me because some will get offended immediately and not hear the real critique, the call to do better. My sorrow on these matters has caused me tears on some occasions, and those tears have given me power to move forward. These same sorrows have also caused others to moan and wonder why the call for assistance went lacking. I begin with **fraternities.**

When I was in college, I thought I wanted to be a "frat man." I'd see them when they were on line and man, they looked good! I began to ask questions about what you had to do to become a member. Most of them really couldn't tell me, they just said if I could get the money, then they could get me in, if I had the grades to qualify.

My interest faded when I saw them at times not able to walk properly. I later learned that they had been hazed. Still later I looked at some of their arms and saw that they had been branded. I saw others taking their dirty laundry to pledges so that they could wash them. They were just doing crazy things, to me, nothing constructive. I saw members, so-called big brothers, cracking eggs on the heads of those being initiated, having them eat raw onions-it did not make sense to me that guys would submit to these kinds of things just to belong.

When I looked down the hill to Plum Street, or Cross Street, or Low Street where people need help to make it and this was what these intelligent, young men were engaging in, it saddened my heart. There were elderly men and women who needed someone to cut their wood for their stoves; others needed help making up their beds, children needed breakfast foods, or that egg that was cracked over another person's head, my sorrow increased. All of those things seemed more important than having your arm branded.

Then a few years ago, Fenton Bland, Jr. who at the time was the State Delegate for the 63rd District (VA, Democrat) , asked me to go to Virginia State University to address an undergraduate chapter of the Kappa's, once again my heart was saddened. I agreed to go and the meeting was being held in Foster Hall. There were about 26 well groomed young men waiting to hear from me. But before I shared my small speech, I asked them, "How many of you are registered to vote?" Only three hands were raised in response to my question! I thought to myself, "What a pity!" How could this be?

Then I recalled a meeting I attended in Atlanta in 1963. Dr. King was very concerned about all of the young people who were in jail and needed bail or bond money to get out. He wrote his fraternity (The Alpha's), other fraternities and sororities, and the Masons begging them for financial support because these youngsters needed to be free. All during July, he constantly asked his secretary, Dora McDonald, had any response came from these organizations and all month she quietly said, "No, response Dr. King." He was so disappointed that I saw him cry for the first time. During that session he said that 'perhaps they have outlived their relevancy'. I think from that moment on he disassociated himself from the Masons, the fraternities, and the sororities. It has been said, "Some members of the fraternities and sororities will not go anywhere with their church, but will go everywhere with their Greek brothers and sisters." So, that's my sorrow. Now let me tell you about an unforeseen joy.

Emma

In 1964, while working in Edenton, North Carolina, Golden Finks and I were going door to door doing a voter registration drive. As we canvassed the community, we found many high school students who were without work and enlisted their aide to complete our task. They were eager to contribute to the struggle and their energy was a joy to behold.

We met this young lady, a recent high school grad, who had no intention of going to college. We were told that she was a smart young woman who just wanted to find a job and get on with her life. She was not an attractive girl and even allowed the other students to call her "monkey." I could not stomach that and refused to do that. When asked had she considered going to college, her response was "No, I have no money. I just want a job." I thought that it would be such a waste of a good mind not to try to go to college and I told her so. Therefore, I said to her, "If we find the money, will you go?"

Now her self esteem was very low and she didn't think much of her chances of succeeding. She was ashamed of where she lived because there was no wood flooring in the kitchen, only the ground! When we came by to pick her up, she was always outside and up the street from where she lived to give the appearance that she stayed somewhere other than her home.

But after a while she agreed that if we found the money she would at least give it a chance. That's all we needed to know. We asked the Masonic groups and graduate chapters of fraternities and sororities in the area for assistance, but no response came forth. But at the mass meetings we'd ask the crowd if they would help in this cause and received enough to at least enroll her in Elizabeth City State Teacher's College! Dr. Walter Ridley, President of Elizabeth City State College, was very helpful in seeing that scholarship aide was also granted.

Immediately, after Labor Day, she went off to enroll at the college and I did not see her again for 30 plus years. But as fate would have it, we met again at a funeral I attended in Washington, D.C. many years later. I had been invited to James

(Jim) Boone's funeral by the family to give some remarks representing what we call the best high school class of Peabody High (Class of 1951). I was traveling with Floyd Henderson, his wife Irma and his sister so I was sensitive to their schedule and was heading back to the car after the funeral was over.

As I walked, a woman (Emma) called out to me, "Mr. Coulton, do you have a moment?" Well, I really didn't know who she was, but paused to hear her. She then began to talk. "We met in North Carolina and you haven't seen me in over 35 years. I am from Edenton and I was your friend, Mr. Boone's, principal. I recently received my doctoral degree and I am so glad to see you." Something clicked when she said, 'doctoral degree' and I asked, "Are you Emma?" She said, "Yes, I am" and we just hugged and cried tears of joy! She would not stop thanking me for believing in her and all that, but I was just so pleased that her mind, and evidently a good one, had not been wasted! This just goes to show that when one door is closed to you, don't quit; there are always people willing to help if you just ask!

The Elks

In 1965, Mr. Henry Harrison, a former neighbor of mine from Harrison St. and a person I had grown to admire, was once again asking me to join the Elks. I had recently got married and so I told my wife that I was going to the Elk's Club on Byrne St. to join. I had already completed the necessary steps in order to "ride the goat" and was looking forward to becoming a member. After my initiation was over, I was told to come to the next month's meeting. My excitement was growing as I was the only new person to join, but another man, John Edmonds, was coming back to be re-instated.

When the next month arrived, I went to the club house expecting the meeting but was told, "No meeting tonight young blood." I noticed that they were drinking at the bar and appearing to be having a good time. I went home and came back the next month and was told again, "No meeting tonight."

Living the rest of your life for the glory of God will require some changes in your priorities, your schedules, your relationships, and everything else. It might even require you to choose a more challenging path rather than an easy one. My soul was troubled and I knew that joining the Elks was not the right thing for me to do. I have always believed that 'I could do badly by myself', I didn't need others to do it for me. Maybe when Mr. Harrison joined the Elks, the organization was something different, something that one could be proud to belong to, but not what I experienced. And then, there were the **Masons**.

Masons

I have had many friends over the years who were members of the various Masonic Lodges of Virginia. Mr. George Vaughan, who married my cousin Rosa, was a well respected member of the Community and a highly esteemed Mason by other masons and me personally. He was the sort of fellow that many men admired and spoke well of, both privately and publicly. He was one of the primary reasons that I was interested in becoming one, to tell you the truth. But the Masons did not solicit new members; you had to enquire about them for yourself.

So, as my interest was growing, I asked a member, "Why are you separated from the white lodges"? I had observed that, like other organizations, segregation existed in the Temples (Halifax St. for blacks and Sycamore St. for whites) but wondered if this was systemic or just social. He never addressed my question. However in fairness, I don't know why I would think that any social group, of the era, would openly flaunt the mores of the Community if the church did not. And while I have seen churches hold integrated special events, I have yet to see black and white Masons meet together.

There's an old saying: 'Masons will help you talk down on the church but will get angry if you spoke against the Masons'. While serving as President of the Virginia Chapter of SCLC, I made the comment that all of the civic and social organizations need to do more to help the Community. This was said at a public gathering and I was asked to come to the Temple and explain what I meant. I went to the meeting and repeated my statement, "All civic and social organizations need to do more"!

Recently I read that a lodge was donating $250.00 as a scholarship to a young woman who was going to college and were celebrating this achievement. That's not enough to cover the cost of books! If that's all you have to give, then do so quietly and without fanfare. But the activity that really irritates me is that when the grandmaster enters a house of worship, all in attendance are asked to stand. I cannot and will not do this. Some may say that I am being petty because I will stand when asked to honor the bride at a wedding, but something in me resents the arrogance of the whole matter. My point, in these sorrows, is that all of these organizations have good principles but I want them to be better. I want them to strive for excellence and they appear to be settling for mediocrity!

Chapter 6:

Appointments

...And some of my thoughts on Virginia's Governors.

"It is an error to suppose that a man belongs to himself. No man does. He belongs to his wife, or his children, or his relations, or to his creditors, or to society in some form or other." G.A. Sala

Appointed to a four year term as a member of the Virginia Parole Board by then Governor Mark Warner, we posed for this photo in the Executive Mansion. (Personal photograph of Herb Coulton)

In 1989, my good friend Hermanze Fauntleroy had been appointed by **Governor Gerald Baliles** to a 4 year term on the *Council of Human Rights* and when his term ended, I succeeded him. My selection occurred under **Governor L. Douglas Wilder**, and this was a 4 year term. In all, Governor Wilder appointed 10 persons to the Council on Human Rights, but the General Assembly never provided us the resources needed to do the job. In fact, many say the only reason Virginia had the council was so that it would not be listed with Mississippi, the last state to form a Council on Human Rights!

Nevertheless, **Zeke Ellison** was appointed Chairman of the Council (by the Governor), we held our meetings regularly, and did very little else. There were many complaints/problems to be addressed but not enough people to visit the job sites to actually confront the matter. In fact, many times the only action taken was a telephone call, rarely was there a follow-up.

My appointment occurred near the end of Governor Wilder's term and carried over into the next administration, that of **Gov. George Allen**. At our annual convention, it was proper protocol to invite the new governor as the keynote speaker, and we did. Governor Allen gave a brief speech, about five minutes in duration, and then asked us after dinner how did we like it (the speech).

In addition, he wanted to meet each council member because he had not appointed any of us. So he was going from table to table, introducing himself or rather reading the name tags, and asking us about the speech. Well, Maxcine was worried I might say how I really felt and suggested, "Herbert, when he comes to this table, please don't say anything to him." I think she meant, be diplomatic and not speak my mind. But I said, "Max, if he comes over here and ask me how I liked the speech, I feel I have an obligation to tell him the truth." I knew that he would come to our table because there were 3 black men and 1 black woman on the Council and that he did not know any of us. He looked at my name tag and said, "So you are Herbert V. Coulton. What does the "V" stand for?" I said, "Voter Registration!" He then asked me how I liked his speech. I said to him, "Governor, you really didn't have anything to say…at least you didn't take long in saying it." I knew from his comments that he either did not know anything about human rights or felt this was not the place to speak his mind.

Still, he allowed me to finish my term of four years and I thanked him for the privilege. Since you serve at the pleasure of the Governor, it was gracious of him. So after my term was over, I thought I would 'sail off into the sunset' and enjoy my retirement.

I was doing very little in my retirement and enjoying every minute of doing nothing. But **Fenton Bland, Jr**. had other ideas. First he called me to ask if I'd be interested in serving on the Virginia Parole Board. I told him, "No!" I saw him during the week and he asked me again and again I said, "No!" So he said he would need someone to send in a resume` so that the governor's staff could recommend a person to the governor for the position, and hopefully from the Petersburg area. At that I told him I would think about it.

Another two weeks passed and he called again. I was sitting on my couch and he asked me had I sent in the requested information? I said that I had not and he said, "Mr. Coulton, please send your information in so that you may be at least considered." So I said I would, hoping that would be the end of the matter.

Three weeks passed and Max and I were sitting at the dinner table eating when the telephone rang. When I answered the phone, the Secretary of the Commonwealth said, "Mr. Coulton, we would like to interview you for a position on the Virginia Parole Board. Can you come to the Capital Building this Wednesday at 2:00 p.m.?" I said I would be there.

I was interviewed by **John Marshall, Secretary of Safety**, and one of his associates for about 55 minutes. John Marshall is the son of former Supreme Court **Justice Thurgood Marshall** and I was deeply impressed.

In March, I received a letter from **Governor Mark Warner** indicating I had been selected to serve a 4 year term as a part-time board member. There are 5 persons on the *Virginia Parole Board*, 3 full time positions and 2 part time positions. One person is also designated the Chairperson, by the Governor, and this position went to **Helen Fehey**, of Arlington, VA. We elected **David Harker** from Forest to the position of Vice Chair and **Carol Sievers** of Newport News to serve as the Victim's Advocate; **Michael Hass** of Elliston and I were the part timers.

Perhaps the governor chose Helen as Chair because she was an attorney but I have always felt that David Harker was more knowledgeable than any of us. After all, he had served as a parole examiner for 25 years and gained immeasurable experience dealing with the system. But then maybe I am biased because David and I developed a close friendship.

Often we ate lunch together, went to meetings together, and I even invited him to come worship with me at First Baptist. He would come! At one of our Veteran's Day Services he shared passionately about an aspect of his personal life and it moved the members deeply. You see he was a former prisoner of war and in sharing that experience, the soul of the man was revealed and he was at peace with himself and the world.

As we were introduced to parole examiners, I asked the Lord for three things: compassion, a forgiving spirit, and common sense. To this day I believe that you need those in abundance if you're to be a good parole board member. There is so much that goes on in the sessions and because I have taken an oath, there are some things I am not at liberty to reveal but I can speak about the personal support they gave me during an illness.

In September, 2004, I had agreed to take a dear friend, **Eventon (Goody) Goodridge** to MCV Hospital for some tests at noon. I had seen my own physician earlier in the day for my own battery of tests at Southside Regional Hospital and because he did not tell me to wait around for the results, I left.

Well Goody and his wife, Lavern, came by my house because they wanted me to drive the vehicle to the hospital in Richmond. When I arrived at the hospital, there was a note at the receptionist's desk for me. It was from Maxcine and read, "Herbert, please check yourself into an emergency room." I really didn't understand the note. I had brought Goody and Lavern to Richmond and I could not leave them there. So after his tests, we headed back to Petersburg.

When I got home, the garage door opened without me using my remote and Maxcine was agitated. "Did you get my note? You need to go to the emergency room now!" She had already called the emergency crew and within 5 minutes they came for me. I had a blockage and they would have to perform surgery. This was Friday, Labor Day weekend, and on Sunday I was at Chippenham Hospital in Richmond where, on Thursday, they performed the open heart surgery.

Once I was released from the hospital, I thought about resigning from the parole board because I was uncertain of the length of my recovery time prior to returning to duty. But John Marshall, the Secretary of Public Safety, visited me and assured me that I could take all the time I needed. His empathy touched me and that spirit spread through the board as well. They were very cooperative in seeing that my cases were managed in my absence.

Even the support staff was exceptional in their willingness and ability to assist you with the work of the board. The staff members I am referring to were **Joan Wade**, **Gloria Cormier**, **Fern Anderson**, and **Laura Hall**. They combined with Desk Top Support, **Arleathia Hillard**, and went beyond the call of duty in their helpfulness. At times, Arleathia acted as my personal "tech support" person in regards to my computer. Sometimes she talked me through the problem on the telephone while at other times I would take my lab top to her, but she was always able to correct the problem for me. I am grateful for their help and support they gave me. Thanks guys!

I returned to work in early 2005 and completed my full term in January 2006. Usually, if you have done a good job and a democrat won the election, you could be asked to stay. If a republican won, then normally new persons would be selected to serve in those positions. So when **Timothy Kaine** was elected Governor, he decided to re-appoint all five of us, which would allow us to serve together until 2009.

I made an honest effort to perform my duties for the parole board but after my heart surgery, my legs did not cooperate with me. It was, and is, very difficult for me to get from the parking lot to the building and then to the office. So I wrote Governor Kaine and thanked him for the re-appointment but regretfully, I resigned in October 2006.

The Virginia Parole Board is very serious work. Sometimes I came home stressed to my limits. I recall that at one meeting I felt compelled to remind my colleagues, "Please remember, we are a parole board not a rejection board!" I felt this was one of the most conservative boards since Virginia began having them and often I was frustrated by many of its decisions. I cannot say more because my term does not expire until 2009 and I am bound by an oath not to give specifics on cases I heard, information I was made aware of, or decisions we made as a Board.

The Virginia Parole Board (Michael Hass, Carol Sievers, David Harker, Secretary of Safety John Marshall, Helen Fehey, and Herbert Coulton) Photo owned by Herb Coulton

Virginia's Governors have been both allies and hindrances to the progressive movements of their day and I would like to say a few things in closing this work. I have been privileged to have known some of them and very briefly, I'd like to share some impressions those made upon me.

Mills Goodwin was a Democrat and served from 1966 until 1970. A group of us from several civil rights organizations met with him in an attempt to get his support for appointing black judges in our state. We spoke for nearly an hour and finally I noticed that he continually referred to us as "Niggras" (Sic) rather than Negroes. Each time he used that term I wrote it down and finally I raised my hand and said to him, "Governor, are you having a problem pronouncing the word Negro because you have said Niggra as if you just cut short of calling us Nigger?" He retorted, "I didn't say that word"! I said, I am sorry, "That's what you said because I wrote it down every time it came out." He turned red as a beet and the meeting was over because he was not going to appoint a black person as a judge anyway. *As a footnote, he changed his party affiliation and ran again in 1974 as a Republican and won!*

Linwood Holton was a pleasant surprise! He served from 1970-74, during Court ordered desegregation in Richmond's Public Schools. But while a candidate for the office he took his children to the public schools where the black kids were enrolled. And although he was a Republican, this demonstrative act of his won my vote! He has been the only Republican I have voted for. He was a fair minded man and turned out to be a good governor.

Charles Robb was governor from 1982-86 and I think he did a good job. After he was elected, his wife Linda Johnson Robb wrote me a letter inviting me to their home in Reston, Virginia. I thought this was rather strange and said to Maxcine that this was a fundraiser. She said, "Why don't you call her?" I did and Mrs. Robb answered the phone and I asked her if in fact this was a fundraiser? Her response caught me off guard. No, it was not a fundraiser but rather an observance of the Voting Rights Bill that her father, **President Lyndon Johnson**, had signed some 35 years ago! She said that she had read that I played a part in getting people registered to vote and they wanted me to be there. In attendance at the dinner was her mother, Former Fisrt Lady "Lady Bird" Johnson, the wife of the late Supreme Court Justice Thurgood Marshall, and perhaps 50 other people. The Governor spoke at the affair and seemed very sincere in his remarks.

Gerald Baliles appointed my friend Hermanze Fauntleroy to the *Council on Human Rights.* Until that appointment, I had not heard of that Council. Perhaps there had been other blacks on that Council but I don't know, I had heard of it. I think Baliles did try to be fair minded, for what its worth. We met with him at least once.

Herbert Coulton with Governor Lawrence D. Wilder

Lawrence Douglas Wilder was a good governor. He was tough minded, but fair. Many groups met with him and I think he attempted to honor most of their requests. I don't know much about his tenure as Mayor of Richmond, but as a governor, I gave him high marks.

James Gilmore met with us as we discussed promotions in the National Guard. He was photographed pinning the star on Brigadier General Bert Holmes, an alumnus of VSU, prior to our meeting and we were hopeful. Unfortunately, this appears like window treatment now because I believe more should have and could have, been done about promotions in the lower ranks.

Chapter 7:
Unsung Heroes

"The idol of today pushes the hero of yesterday
out of our recollection;
And will, in turn, be supplanted
by his successor of tomorrow."
Washington Irvington

There are so many people who have made significant contributions towards making this journey bearable. Some were never recognized while others have gone on to their final resting place. But for me, there are some heroes in my life that I would like to speak briefly about. Naturally, once you start calling names someone will be forgotten, but here's a few that stand out in my mind.

Victoria Jackson Gray Adams was one of the 'Queens' of the Civil Rights Movement. I first met her in 1964 at SCLC's Dorchester Citizenship training program in Hinesville, Georgia. She was one of the instructors teaching literacy courses to adults unable to read or write. I was impressed with her passion for her work and the results they were able to accomplish. I didn't know of her involvement with the Mississippi Freedom Democratic Party (MFDP) at the time because she didn't wear it as a badge of honor, but 'Vicky' was special.

In addition to being a co-founder of the party with Fannie Lou Hamer, she was the first woman to run for the United States Senate from Mississippi; not first black woman, but the first woman period! And although she lost to the incumbent, John Stennis, the message was sent to the power structure that change was in the air. Later, after registering more than 80, 000 Black Mississippians to vote in straw polls, her delegation challenged the seating of the Mississippi delegation to the Democratic National Convention in Atlantic City (1964), demonstrating that since Mississippi practiced illegal voting practices, the delegation could not possibly represent the citizens of Mississippi! She lost that scrimmage but in 1968, they again challenged the practice in Chicago and won the war. The Democratic Convention recognized their integrated group as the delegation from Mississippi. Along with Fannie Lou Hamer and Annie Devine, Vicky was one of the first three African American women in the history of the United States to be seated as guests of honor on the floor of the U.S. Senate. Now is that special or what?

When we next got together again, it was at Fort Myers (Virginia) where I was visiting my brother Marvin, who was stationed there. She and her husband, Reuben, were living next door to him. (How small is this world?) Then she shocked me again by moving to Petersburg.

As Reuben was getting close to retirement, the Army sent him to Ft. Lee and after retirement, they settled here. He is an accomplished chef and was immediately hired in Food Services by Virginia State University, while she became active in the Community. They purchased the former parsonage of Gillfield Church on Dunlop Street and became immersed in the life of the city.

Vicky was a gem. She was always open to suggestions and if you had anything constructive to do in the community, she would help you do it. I became better acquainted with her when she began the Campus Ministry at Virginia State University.

As a life long member of the United Methodist Church, she was persuasive in getting the Virginia Annual Conference, in conjunction with the Presbyterian Church, USA, to begin a ministry to the students of VSU. Initially, she was doing this on a part-time basis and didn't even have an office on Campus. Yet she would organize events and bring in speakers to attempt to make a difference in the lives of the young adults. When Rev. Daniely came to VSU, they found each other and worked to make the ministry an integral part of campus life.

About that time, I joined the Board of Directors and we worked together to bring others from the Community to the table in support of this effort. When the ministry was about to became a full time matter, she graciously stepped aside and allowed Daniely to run with it.

Meanwhile, she was still serving on the state SCLC Board and we were involved with the Community Bank. This bank was not responsive to our request for diversity on its board, so we decided to protest their offices and bring attention to the matter. Vicky was ill and hid the magnitude of her illness from us. If I had known the gravity of her illness, I never would have asked her to join our picket line. When I suggested that perhaps she should stay away, she would say, "Now Herb, I am not so sick that I can't lend a helping hand." Vicky died in 2006.

William J. Alexander was a large man physically and in his personal character. In addition, he was proud to tell anyone listening that he was from Brunswick County. Many years ago, when I was a youngster, he began a school bus line so that he could give black kids a ride to school because there was no transportation for them. The county provided buses for the white kids only and he thought a bus service should be available to the black kids as well. The county did not think so!

He tells the story that he started his formal education at age 22 because as the oldest of 12 siblings, he wanted them to be educated before him. This gives us a glimpse into the man but allow me to say more. Although he entered school late, he was self educated, the "self-made man," if you will.

He was often the butt of jokes, but he did not care. In fact, when he relocated to Petersburg, his house was called the 'leaning shack' because he built it himself and it was actually leaning. He did all the work, by himself! Carpentry, electrical, plumbing, everything was done by him. He was unorthodox, but he was sincere.

Mr. Alexander was a strong proponent of the ballot and a staunch supporter of Dr. King, Rev. Wyatt T. Walker, and Rev. Grady Powell (his 'homeboy' and the esteemed pastor of

Gillfield Baptist Church). Many times when his old car would not run, you could see him walking, carrying his registration materials in Petersburg or his beloved County. He would not accept the excuse that his car didn't run when people needed the information he had to share! Once, when he came by the SCLC office in Petersburg, I noticed that his shoes were worn out. He was literally walking on the sides of the shoes and I asked him could we take him to get some shoes for his feet. He refused us initially because he felt he needed to get back to his county immediately because a family was waiting for him to bring them the registration materials! I told him that I would take him to Brunswick County if he would just allow me to buy him some shoes first. His comment was, "Alright, but hurry up Coulton!" We went to several stores in Petersburg but they didn't have his size, 13E. Finally, we went to Richmond and were able to get the shoes and then we took him home.

On his 85th birthday, William N. Bland, Sr. of Bland's Funeral Home, and I purposed to honor him with a birthday party. Bland said Mr. Alexander had never had a birthday party and suggested that we give him one. We wanted to invite his family but we didn't know them.

Mr. Alexander was living in Sycamore Towers by then and we received the manger's permission to have the gathering there. Most of his family was deceased but we were able to locate one sister and began asking about other living relatives. While he listened in, he heard this sister say, "I'm not coming to Petersburg to a party for Ole Alex" and it broke his heart. It also destroyed the spirit of the party! What irony that a man who would walk all over Virginia to help others register to vote was not esteemed enough in his sister's eyes that she would ride to Petersburg to share in a party with him.

James Canady and I met around 1949 at the home of John Edmonds on Crater Road. My friend, Clifton (Peter) Jones lived next door to John and they were planning a trip to the cannery in Lawrenceville, where apples were canned. Jim, a native of North Carolina, was still in the military and had stopped by with his Army buddy, Robert (Bob) Daughtry, whom I knew from my days of summer work at the apple orchid near Jones Lake. (Bernard Lundy and James Parham also worked there with us during the summer months).

As a result of President Harry Truman's Executive Order to integrate the military, change was in the air. However, change at the southern bases was at a crawl, if at all. Black and white soldiers lived in separate barracks, which made total integration impossible. When Jim arrived at **Camp Lee (now Ft. Lee)** as a part of the medical corps, blacks could not even drive the ambulances!

After several years in Petersburg, he married the love of his life, Jean, and was sent to France (1952), where two of his children were born. Jim had a gift for languages and became fluent in French, which served him well as an interpreter later in life. So after a several assignments stateside, (Kansas, Missouri, NC), a tour of Vietnam (1st Division), Germany, and a second tour of France, Jim retired from the military in 1967.

He and his wife, Jean, returned to Petersburg in 1981 as a civilian, and was now in his second career- that of civil service. Prior to returning to Petersburg, his Civil service career had taken him to Ft. Bragg (NC) and Ft. Riley (Kansas) where he managed the base laundry and did an outstanding job. Interestingly enough, he returned to Ft. Lee as the Equal Opportunity Officer!

Perhaps he was most proud of his work with veterans, assisting them to receive their hard earned benefits. The process of leaving the military can be stressful and the exit interviews less than fully transparent. In other words, important information was sometimes glossed over and left to the individual to discover on their own. Unfortunately, this was common place and those least educated, black or white, were often the ones who suffered. Well this quiet man, though short of statute, was a giant in assisting veterans to learn what benefits they were entitled to and how to apply for them. He also later served as Chairman of the Board of the Virginia State SCLC. As a servant of humanity and of God, I say, "Well done." (Jim died March 8, 2009, but his legacy lives on!)

Marie Coone once said of her own self, "As a result, I am what I am by the grace of God-confident, competent, resilient, optimistic, with abiding faith, a love for people, and a desire to use this one life to create a new and better reality for others."

She was born in Alabama and graduated from Daleville High School where she was the co-editor of the school newspaper. She was a member of the National Honor Society and was voted Most Intellectual Senior Girl. She received her BS degree (Suma Cum Laude) and a Masters from Troy State University, then went on to receive a certificate in Non-profit Management from Virginia Commonwealth University. She was and is a strong advocate for social justice and has always been actively involved in numerous community and professional organizations. In addition, she is a life member of SCLC and the NAACP.

Marie enjoys creative writing and has written and directed several plays including: "What Will Become of My People," "Somehow I Made It," and "By Their Love." Marie was very helpful to the SCLC before and during my tenure as president. I will always be grateful to her steadfast spirit and her attention to detail.

George M. Ellis is another one of the quiet warriors of the movement. When we began, George worked for W. T. Grant's Five & Dime Store. He was a part-time stock clerk in this store that would not allow blacks to eat at its lunch counter. We attempted to negotiate in good faith with the management but to no avail, so we decided to hold sit-ins.

The manager told George to rope off the lunch counter so that we could not sit down and George refused to do so. In fact, he told the manager if he wanted the counter roped off, he would have to do it himself. Then he walked off the job in protest! This was no small matter because George needed the small amount of money he was earning. This was a courageous act and demonstrated his commitment to what we were attempting to accomplish. Most people don't know that about

George and I think he should be saluted. How many of you would walk away from a job out of protest concerning social issues?

But he was always concerned about the welfare of others, not just himself. In fact, in spite of his heavy involvement with the Masons (I try not to hold that against him) he was dedicated to the end. He became a member of the state board of SCLC and has continued his service to the cause and to the community.

At another level, and perhaps a greater one, he and his wife, Lessie, should win the grandparents of the year award. They are presently raising four grandchildren. I don't mean caring for them after school and then sending them home. I mean these children live with them on a daily basis. I visit them occasionally and am amazed by what I observe. These kids are well mannered, respectful, and doing well in school. I tip my hat to them. There are not many of us seniors raising their grandchildren alone.

Dr. Florence Farley is a native of Roanoke but has made Petersburg her home. After graduating from Virginia State College (now VSU) with a Bachelor's in Psychology, she returned home and taught in a private school. Then, as a result of President Harry Truman's Executive Order to integrate the Armed Services, she applied and was accepted as a 2nd Lieutenant in a special program to help the transition, the Women's Army Corp WAC's). As one of five black officers (out of 110) she learned anew the depths of racial prejudice and bigotry.

After serving 3 years in the military, she resigned her commission and with the support of the G.I. Bill, entered graduate school at Virginia State as a full time student in Educational Psychology. Her mentor was a Harvard grad, Dr. Keturah Whitehurst, who taught her the rudiments of Clinical Psychology because VSC didn't offer that program and upon completion of her program, she was also ready to do what she was called to do. Therefore upon receiving her Master's Degree, she was admitted into an internship at Crownsville State Mental Hospital for Blacks (MD.). (Virginia didn't offer a program in Clinical Psychology for blacks!)

As a by-product of the two Supreme Court rulings, (Brown vs. Board of Education Supreme Court, 1954 and the 1955 expansion to 'move with all deliberate speed'), states had to integrate all aspects of education; she was hired at Central State Hospital in May of 1955. This state run facility, the first state supported hospital in the nation for black patients, served only black patients but all the professional staff was white. As the first black professional at Central State, she created a dilemma for the administration.

They had a separate cafeteria for those black people working at the hospital, which was located in the basement of one of the buildings, but Florence would not eat there. So she went to the better cafeteria, reserved for whites only and although it was unusual, for about 8 weeks she was able to eat her meals comfortably. Then a complaint was filed with the governor's office and it was decided that in an era of State's Rights, this would not be tolerated. A private dining area was set up for her, and any guest she might want to bring with her, but she could no longer eat in the lunch area previously reserved for white. Florence protested and refused to eat in this separate facility! Instead, she traveled to VSC and ate in the cafeteria there.

Then she began to chronicle what she saw: dehumanizing conditions for the all black patients, such as having them sleep on the bare floor; and most incriminating, the hospital's main administrative building had one bathroom for all black persons to use, patients, their visitors, all the blacker workers, both males and females. She also noted that black patients were routinely taken off site to work (for free) at the homes and farms of the white staff and she decided that she had had enough.

She arranged for **Rev. Vernon Johns** and David Gunter (President of the NAACP) to observe what she witnessed on a daily basis and together they exposed the racial climate at this facility. How ironic, that this 'sickness' existed at a hospital for the mentally challenged!

For seven (7) years she agitated on behalf of the patients and when the administration decided to re-instate their **Annual Watermelon Pic-Nic** for the black patients, and advertise it in the *Journal for Mental Health* (a statewide publication), she knew it was time to leave.

While having her meals at VSC, she had become active with the Psychology Department, participating in events and forums, and knew many of the students and faculty. She also knew the University's President, **Dr. Robert P. Daniels**, who had taken note of this daughter of Troy, and was interested in hiring her if ever she wanted a position. So she returned to her alma mater as a faculty member and for several years it felt like paradise. Then Dr. Daniels died and things changed abruptly!

First, there was a move afloat to discontinue the Agricultural Department at VSC and enlarge the program at Virginia Tech. This would mean a well established program, and one of the original offerings since 1882 at VSC would be effectively shut down, a few token jobs would be given to black faculty members, and the students would be the ultimate losers; so the students protested! Florence joined their fight and they won.

They won because **Curtis Harris**, who had campaigned successfully for and brought out the black vote for the new governor, Linwood Holton, arranged a meeting for **The Concerned Students and Faculty** so they could present their case to him. This group, three students and two faculty members, of course Florence was one of them, met with the governor on a Saturday morning and shared the successes of the program at VSC and vowed to continue this success if given a chance. Governor Holton was swayed and the program was saved at VSC.

Then, Richard Bland, a junior college in the area, was attempting to become a four year institution. That in itself was not problematic, but the members of the General Assembly, headed by Delegate Roy Smith, were supporting the move, and thereby funding it. This same Assembly had prejudiced itself against Virginia State by its historical actions of underfunding that institution. Therefore to attempt to fully fund a smaller school, whose constituents just happened to be white and in the same community, was tainted with racial undertones. Florence's group, The Concerned Students and Faculty, fought this action.

They protested in the Community, marched in Richmond, and took over 2500 people to the General Assembly to further voice their discontent. Finally, they took the matter to court, all the way to the US Supreme Court. In a Supreme Court ruling, based on the **1965 Civil Rights Act**, the court ruled that Richard Bland could not escalate beyond 200 level classes. In other words, they were chartered as a Junior College and would have to stay that way! But her fighting was not over.

In 1972 Petersburg was able to annex portions of Dinwiddie and Prince George Counties to expand her borders. This also effectively diluted the black vote and made it virtually impossible with an at large system to get representation on City Council. Florence and others fought this as a violation of the **Voting Rights Act**. Once again, the US Supreme Court was supportive in recognizing that this was a measure to ensure blacks had insufficient representation in the Community. Therefore the wards system was mandated for a one year trial to determine if this would open the door to equal representation under the law. It proved a useful tool as for the first time; a woman was elected to the City Council: Florence Farley.

At the same time, Florence, a National Fellow, was continuing her education. During the summers she furthered her training by enrolling in classes at Harvard University and Beloit College (Wisconsin). Kent State University (Akron, Ohio) began an initiative aimed at encouraging faculty members at Historically Black Colleges & Universities (HBCU's) to enter into one of their Ph.D. programs. Florence was encouraged by her department and applied. So in 1975, she took a sabbatical from VSC and enrolled at Kent State. This University offered her the position of assistant professor while she matriculated there, the state of Virginia gave her ½ her salary, and she completed her work in two years! In 1977, armed with her Ph. D. in Educational Psychology, she returned to her alma mater and subsequently served as Departmental Chair. Later, she became he first black female Mayor in the Commonwealth of Virginia. Florence will forever be in the trenches.

Hermanze & Germaine Fauntleroy: an excellent example of persons making sacrifices for the welfare of the larger Community as we began our struggle for human dignity and freedom. This couple made personal and professional sacrifices during the early days of the movement that are worthy of mention. Before he was elected as the Mayor of Petersburg, the first African American in the Commonwealth of Virginia to be so honored, Hermanze and his wife were teachers in the Petersburg Public School system. They would finish their days work, go home to feed their three daughters, and then join the picket lines most evenings. Following a strong desire to effect change in his community, Hermanze decided to run for public office, City Council, and continue the struggle at another level.

Therefore in 1966, he ran for an at large seat on the City Council and won. At the time, and unknown to him, there was a statute prohibiting him from being on the Council and maintaining his position as a teacher. After being sworn in as a City Council member, he was informed, the following morning, that not only could he not continue to teach but that he had to leave the school facility and not have any contact with his students. (John Meade, the School Superintendent in Petersburg, had to confer with the Attorney General before making this decision.)

What a dilemma! It appeared to us that he was being penalized for his involvement with the movement; but the law is the law! Yet he still had three little girls to take care of and now he had to attempt this with less money, all while being away from home more because of his civic responsibility. Still, at least publicly he didn't complain; instead, very stoically he responded, "Herb, I owe that much to the people who elected me." Perhaps God smiled upon his resolve and blessed him because he served as Mayor from 1973-74 and again from 1976-80. That statute has since been overturned and although Hermanze suffered financially because of it, others don't have that burden to deal with.

Germaine, his devoted and supportive wife, was also a brilliant woman! We took several classes together and I can attest to it personally. Floyd Jackson also was at VSU at the same time and he affectionately called her "computer brain." She received her bachelor's degree and two Masters from VSU and then her Ph.D. from VCU (Virginia Commonwealth University). She has served as the principal of Petersburg High School and was the first female to serve as the Superintendent of the Petersburg Public School System! She is to be admired for her accomplishments as well as her steadfast support of her husband.

David Gunter: was the Food Service Manager at VSU, but much more. I first met him in our old PIA (Petersburg Improvement Association) office at 244 Halifax Street. He came by, introduced himself, and wanted to help. He asked if we needed more students because he wanted to get the students of VSU involved in the struggle.

I accompanied him to Campus and witnessed him standing on the tables in Jones Dining Hall and encouraging, enlisting, and inviting the students to get "involved in the revolution going on in Petersburg." The students enthusiastically responded to his plea and hundreds of them walked to the PIA office that day. And they did not stop coming because he repeated his 'call to action' on a regular basis. There are many staff persons working today at VSU who still vividly recall his antics and are glad that he was there and able to motivate them to join the cause. Most would not have confronted the power structure without his impetus.

A vivid example of this was Dr. George Washington "Kid" McLaughlin, college professor by day, but taxi cab driver in the evenings and on weekends. He would insist upon giving free rides to the student participants. He thought that the cab company should transport the students to Petersburg to picket and then back to Campus. It was his way of contributing to the movement because, in his words, "I am not non-violent, but I support what you are doing."

But David was more than an impetus for the students and the faculty; he was also a motivator for us. One day, as we were taking a break, we went over to Fauntleroy's home to relax a little and I witnessed another side to this passionate man. He began to recite Shakespeare's Macbeth and was so moved by the words that he began to cry! I said to him, "David, do it again!" He said, "Give me a minute or two to gather myself." Once he had collected himself, he recited it again, this time better than before! We had never heard such power, sensitivity, and clarity. There were not that many blacks in movies or show business and none moved us like he did that Thursday afternoon. We all said that he had missed his calling. What would have happened if he had a sponsor or benefactor? We'll never know, but I do know that without him, the students of VSU would not have been as involved in the struggle as they were. He was a wonder to behold.

Rev. Clyde Johnson came into my life some forty years ago when he was called as Pastor to the historic First Baptist Church of Petersburg. It was in March, 1968, just a few weeks before the assassination of Dr. Martin. Luther King, Jr.

On the night of Dr. King's death, a special service was being held at First Baptist; even while plans were being made for several of us to travel to the funeral. Rev. Johnson, as Pastor, headed the delegation which included Mr. William Bland (Bland's Funeral Home), Ms. Cassie Walker (The Little Lady Beauty Salon), Mr. Edward B. Farley (teacher from Dinwiddie's Public Schools) and me, bound for Atlanta.

It was only after our return from Atlanta that I learned of his involvement in the movement. You see, as a student and then as a young Pastor (First Baptist Church of Weldon), Rev. Johnson had participated in student sit-ins at Shaw University. The KKK had even burned a cross on the Church's lawn during a civil rights meeting, but he was not deterred. In fact, it might have made him more committed.

As providence would have it, Rev. Johnson was totally oblivious of the history of First Baptist's involvement in the Movement. Some 20 years prior to his arrival, Rev. Milton Reid ran for the office of State Senator. In addition, Rev. Reid served as campaign manger for Deacon Joseph Owens successful campaign for City Council; making him the first African American to serve on Petersburg's City Council since Reconstruction!

Then, with the coming of the Ward System in 1973, Rev. Johnson took up the mantle, won a seat on Council (6th Ward) and with Dr. Florence Farley, Hermanze Fauntleroy, and Roy Hines, formed the first African American majority on Council. He served the city and the 6th Ward for 13 years and I was his campaign manger for two of his four terms.

As the Director of SCLC, we journeyed together many times in fulfilling our obligations. It was not uncommon for him to leave the pulpit and travel with me to Prince George or Waverly to feed the hungry, or engage in other activities to uplift our people or fan the flames of hope.

In addition, he was a good steward/leader at First Baptist. For example, under his watch: a huge debt was liquidated, a new heating system was installed, additional property was purchased, and in cooperation with the trustees, stain glass windows were installed, chimes were added to our organ, and a new educational wing was constructed. Several organizations were established, including the Male Chorus and the Gospel Choir.

During Rev. Johnson's untimely arrest and subsequent imprisonment, only a few 'men of the cloth' supported him during this ordeal. What I am speaking to is not about innocence or guilt, but compassion. They forget the words of Jesus, recorded in the 25th Chapter of Matthew's Gospel. There, you find these words beginning at verse 42, *"for I was hungry and you gave me no food, I was thirsty and you gave me nothing to drink, I was a stranger and you did not welcome me, naked and you did not give me clothing, sick and in prison and you did not visit me. Then he will answer them, 'Truly I tell you, just as you did not do it to one of the least of these, you did not do it to me.' " (New Revised Standard)* How sad, a brother in need of compassion and they judged him unworthy of God's grace.

When my wife and I visited Rev. Johnson, he always lifted our spirits. He was always upbeat and positive about the future because he believed that God would deliver him. In fact, he stayed busy preaching and teaching fellow prisoners.

He was allowed to hold revival services while incarcerated. He found favor with the guards and the warden, wherever he went. I remember the words of Joseph, when he was speaking to his brothers, "But as for you, ye thought evil against me; but God meant it unto good, to bring to pass, as it is this day, to save much people alive." (Genesis 50: 20, KJV).

Milton H. Richardson is one of those persons I have admired for many years. He began working with the youth group of the Petersburg Improvement Association (PIA) when he was nine years old. At the time, the Director was Mrs. Bessie Reid Jones a teacher in the Petersburg School System. She was a stern disciplinarian and "didn't take no mess" from anyone.

Milton demonstrated a willingness to serve and his attitude was noted. When it was time to picket, he was there. When it became time to participate in sit-ins, he was there! This dedication grew throughout his youth and when he became older, he was given authority over the youth group. He was an integral part of the leadership team and was there at our 'midnight oil' meetings, giving his voice when hard decisions had to be made. As I began writing this, Milton had been hospitalized for several months and I have just received word that he has died (September 26, 2007). May God receive his soul and commend him for his dedication.

Roland Sherrod was one young adult I learned to depend upon. During the 'hey day' of the movement, I relied upon him to help me with the students of Petersburg High School and

VSU as we picketed the stores involved in overt discrimination. Although he was just a little older than they, he always was able to speak a word of calm to them when they got rowdy. In fact, he seemed much older than his age. If I had to leave the community, I knew that he would be able to follow my instructions implicitly. His older brother, Charles, ran the movement in Albany Georgia and perhaps it was in the blood, so to speak, but he was instrumental to our success in Petersburg.

As time went on, he left to join the military. He's retired now and occasionally I still see him. He lives in Richmond where he's the caregiver for his mother.

Cassie L. Walker, owner of the Little Lady Beauty Salon, was more than a beautician. I first met her at a Voter Registration meeting I was conducting in the Blandford Community in 1959. She told me that she was from Whitesville North Carolina and was interested in helping to register blacks to vote. In fact, a constant question to her customers at the salon was, "Are you registered to vote?"

As word spread that we would be holding sit-ins at the Petersburg Public Library, she told her customers, "I will be closed that day. I must be at the library." She joined the group of protesters already assembled, students from Peabody High School and Virginia State College, ministers and others and was ultimately arrested along with the rest of us. After that, she was hooked on the movement.

Soon thereafter, she joined the Petersburg Improvement Association and the SCLC. Fortunately for us, she later became treasurer of the latter and helped us tremendously. Often, when funds were low, she would 'advance' the unit hundreds of dollars saying, "You can pay me back when you can." Then, when we had the money, she would not take it.

She did similar charitable deeds in the Community, helping students without the means to go to college. She wanted to help, but did not want to be recognized for doing so. She would say to me, "Now Coulton, don't you say anything about my giving these children money for school."

During the summer months, she would see to it that many of the students arrived to our office early. Sometimes she even set her appointments aside and drove them to 244 Halifax Street. And during the holidays, she would send boxes of perishable and non perishable food to help the meet the needs of the growing list of persons requesting holiday baskets. That's the kind of woman she was, always looking for ways to help someone else.

When Dr. King was murdered, she called our office to find out if there was any way that she could be included in the group going to Atlanta. Although she was not fond of flying, she thought this would allow us to arrive on time. She even offered to provide transportation to the airport for the group. Although we did not need that because Nelson Bland took care of it, the thoughtfulness touched me.

Even when her health began to fail, she always kept in touch to see if there was anything that she could do to help. We told her, she had done enough and that she needed to take it easy and get well, if possible. She died on March 1, 1989 and most of the movement folk knew that we had lost a real committed sister in the struggle, a champion of the cause for freedom.

John White is a man I wish I had known earlier in life. I first met this man from Emporia when he came to a board meting of the SCLC. At the time, he was President of the Greenville/Emporia Chapter and for some reason, our paths had never crossed. This was especially ironic because his chapter was the most productive chapter of SCLC in the entire state of Virginia. They had more active members numerically and were noted for their support of needy families and school children.

He worked as a Safety Director for the Department of Corrections for many years and presently serves on the Emporia City Council. Even there he's a straight shooter. If he tells you he's going to do something-he'll do it. If he tells you that he'll be at a place, at a particular time- count on it! He epitomizes the slogan: "No man stands taller than when he stoops to help another." I am happy to have met him and to have served the citizens of Virginia with him. My only regret is that I did not meet him sooner.

Carl Winfield began working with the Petersburg chapter of the SCLC when he was 15 years old. I recall that after the March on Washington (1963), he was involved in getting young people to canvass areas of the city, to encourage adults to both pay their poll tax and register to vote! He engaged his sisters, Adelle and Christine, to assist him, working from sun rise to sun set.

Carl was active in the strategy sessions as well as the implementation of policies. So when negotiations with **High's Ice Cream and Liberty Market** broke down over their refusal to hire blacks, he personally recruited students to picket them.

Once the Blue Bird Theatre was finally integrated, Carl was one of the first students to attend a show. When he and Jewel Stewart left the show however, he got a little more than he had bargained for. As they walked along the street, a car stopped and a young white male jumped out of the car and pulled a knife on them. This boy knew they had come from the movie and was probably trying to intimidate them when he shouted, "What you niggers want?" Although the police prevented any violence, you never really know what's in the hearts of people.

When Andy Young called and said Dr. King was coming to Virginia to recruit people for the Poor Peoples Campaign, I asked Carl to start recruiting. He was on top of it and had an extensive list of names. He was looking forward to Dr. King coming to Petersburg and like the rest of us, was heart broken by his death on April 4, 1968. He said, "I am going to take that march to Washington some day." He spoke of it often, like it was a promise to his own self.

On January 5, 2009, he called me and said, "Herb, I have given the thought of marching to Washington a lot of consideration. I have mapped my schedule out and I am going to do it. I'm going to finish what Dr. King couldn't finish. What do you think?" I said, "I think it's great! I only wished my legs were stronger…I'd go with you."

At 7:00 a.m. on Sunday, January 11th, he called again. He said, "Herb, I am in front of the old SCLC office at 244 Halifax Street in Petersburg preparing to begin my march." I had a breakfast meeting, sponsored by the James H. Threatt Memorial Club which was to begin at 7:30 a.m. but I wanted to check on my friend. As soon as the meeting was over, Councilman David Coleman, James Canady, and I left Jones Dining Hall, on the Campus of Virginia State University and went looking for him.

David was driving and we all agreed that he should drive North on Jeff Davis highway and see if we could find Carl. We had gone almost to Bellwood before we spotted him, walking facing the southbound traffic. So we went ahead and turned around so that we'd be on the same side of the street as he was.

He was approaching us, just singing. When he recognized who were, he began laughing. We embraced him and I offered him a little bit of money because I knew he'd get hungry and would need to stop overnight at some motel. He didn't ask us for anything, but I insisted that he take the money. I also encouraged him to be alert and not walk at night. He thanked us for our concern and indicated he would call me that night. Well, he called as he arrived in Fredericksburg, then from Alexandria, and finally from Washington, D.C. Carl said he felt much better after completing the journey-a journey that no on else had done.

Epilogue

"Who has not raised a tombstone, here and there, over buried hopes and dead joys, on the road of life? Like the scars of the heart, they are not to be obliterated."
Ninon de Lenclos

I shall never forget what my friend Samuel Otis Smith so often would say, "We are all going to hell in a hand basket." In a real sense, I think he might be right. How in the world did this country allow that fool in the White House get elected twice?

How did we get so hung up with Michael Vick killing pit bull dogs and then getting arrested when Barbaro, the horse that broke his leg during the Preakness Stakes was killed because he could not win any more races? According to Richard Sandomir, "And we ask them to run-they run- and when they don't, they die!"

The former Beatle Paul McCartney is credited with saying, "If slaughterhouses had glass windows, we'd all be vegetarians."

How can we continue to spend billions of dollars on an unjust war when over 34 million people, in this country, go to bed hungry every night? How many families are there who don't have nor can afford to have adequate health care? How many of their children cannot afford to go to college because they have no money? Why has not only the number of Pell Grants been greatly reduced but also the amount of each grant?

How is it that Rev. Clyde Johnson, who will be getting out of prison soon, not able to find forgiveness among the church community? Are not these the same people who attend church every Sunday, themselves asking God for forgive in their songs and prayers?

Back in, I believe 1968, an incident occurred that I rarely mention. It seems that Lois Walton was missing. I had requested that the men's club at First Baptist Church launch a search party for this young lady. This was a Sunday and they had agreed to help. Later that day I received a call from Petersburg's Police Department asking if they could join in with us. I saw no problem with that and readily agreed because I felt that all concerned citizens should feel free to join us.

Well, we began our search going from First Baptist toward Defense Road. We had no evidence or clues to tell us where to search so when it became dark, we decided to stop for the night. When she was finally found, I received a call the very next day at the old SCLC office. Someone, disguising their voice, said to me, "You keep fooling around with this case and your son might be next."

My son was only four years old and was attending Holy Family Day Care at the time. I immediately went over there, told them about the call and asked them to watch him closely and not reveal to Maxcine what I had said. When my wife came by after work to pick up our son, the staff told her! Of course she became upset and then I became angry myself. In a real sense she needed to know and I felt bad that I had tried to keep it from her when she really did need to be aware of all that was happening. Thanks unto God that Herbert Vanlot Coulton, Jr. is alive and well in spite of dad's ignorance! I don't think I have ever told him, until now.

In April of 2005, I received a letter from **Dr. Eddie Moore,** President of VSU, informing me that I had been chosen to receive a Certificate of Merit. I was honored because after all these years, my alma mater was honoring me**. Mrs. Sandra Garner,** a long time friend, who works at VSU, had submitted the necessary documentation and had not informed me of what she was doing. I am grateful to her.

The certificate reads: "In recognition of his outstanding service to the Commonwealth of Virginia and Virginia State University we award this certificate to Herbert V. Coulton, Sr."

What I really wanted to share is that we are a great people. We as African Americans have done so much when we have had so little to work with! Imagine with me, what we might accomplish now that we have so much more!

Finally, I can remember fondly those rainy days on Old Church Street, with my colleagues, whom I have known from the movement and I have tried to be true to them; especially the precious memories of those no longer here. I have said what I wanted to say and I feel at peace.

Herbert Coulton is standing in hallway, prior to receiving Certificate of Merit from VSU. May 2005
Photo by James G. Daniely

Bibliography

The Collected Poems of Langston Hughes, ed. Arnold Rampersad (New York: Alfred A. Knopf, Inc., 1995).

Holt, Len. An Act of Conscience (Boston: Beacon Press, 1965).

Jones, William A. God In The Ghetto (Elgin, Il: Progressive Publishing, 1979).

Walker, Wyatt. T. Common Thieves (New York: Martin Luther King Fellows Press, 1986)

THE VIRGINIA STATE UNIT OF THE

SOUTHERN CHRISTIAN LEADERSHIP CONFERENCE

Presents

DR. MARTIN LUTHER KING, JR.

in the

EASTERN VIRGINIA MASS MEETING

March 28, 1962 at 8:00 P. M.

at

THE FIRST BAPTIST CHURCH

236 Harrison Street

Petersburg, Virginia

Dr. Milton A. Reid, State President,

S. C. L. C., Minister

Co-Sponsors

The Petersburg Improvement Association

Mr. David Gunter, President

The Hopewell Improvement Association

Reverend Curtis Harris, President

Original program from March 1962

PROGRAM

Dr. Milton A. Reid, President . . . . Presiding
Virginia State Unit of S. C. L. C.

Music . . . . The Goodwill Community Singers

Invocation . . . . Dr. F. J. Boddie Sr., Minister
The Tabernacle Baptist Church

National Athem . . . . Audience Standing
"The Star Spangled Banner"

Scripture . . . . Reverend Grady W. Powell, Minister
I Corinthians 13:1–13 The Gilfield Baptist Church

Prayer . . . . Dr. E. D. Shands, Minister
Bethany Baptist Association

Special Music . . . . Goodwill Chorus

Two Minute Greetings:

Petersburg Improvement Association . . Mr. David Gunter, President

Clergy Representative . . . . Reverend E. E. Hicks, President
Baptist Ministers Conference

Hopewell Improvement Association . . Reverend Curtis Harris, President

Voting Registration . . . . Mr. Herbert Coulton, Field Secretary
S. C. L. C.

N. A. A. C. P. . . . . Dr. L. C. Johnson, President

Youth of the City . . . . Miss Priscilla McLeod

Legal Counselor . . . . Attorney Len Holt
Counsel for State Unit S. C. L. C.

Special Music . . . . Goodwill Chorus

Response . . . . Reverend Wyatt T. Walker
Director of S. C. L. C.

Citizenship School . . . . Mrs. Dorothy Cotton
Educational Consultant

Financial Appeal . . . . Reverend Robert G. Williams, President
Baptist General Association

Reverend Ralph D. Abernathy, Treasurer
S. C. L. C.

Special Music . . . . Goodwill Chorus

Introduction of Speaker . . . . Reverend Virgil A. Wood, Acting Chairman
Board of Directors S. C. L. C.

Address . . . . Dr. Martin Luther King, Jr., President
S. C. L. C., Atlanta, Georgia

Recruitment of
Freedom Corps Volunteers . . . . Reverend Ralph D. Abnerathy

Closing Hymn . . . . Audience Standing
"Lift Every Voice and Sing"

Herb's Surprise 75th Birthday Party 2009!

(All photos by James Daniely)

Floyd Henderson, Irma Henderson, and Deacon Eugene Bland

Maxcine smiles because she pulled off the surprise party!

Below: Mrs. Sue Richardson and Ms. Peggy C. L. Lee

Mrs. Adrian Cook and Mizell Cook (Maxcine's niece and Great niece

The Coulton men: Junior and Senior.

Below: Deacon Joe Moore, Rev. Clyde Johnson, Mrs. Marian Moore, and Mrs. Sue Richardson

All photos this page by James G. Daniely

Mr. Drew Meade (Neighbor), Brittany (Granddaughter), Mrs. Vonda Coulton (Daughter-in-law) and Herb Coulton, Jr. gather to celebrate #75!
Photo by James G. Daniely

Herb & Maxcine:
Renewing Their Vows, 2008!

Photos by James Daniely

Above: Herb and Maxcine renew their vows and Granddaughter Tadia looks on. Dr. Jeremiah Tillman and Rev. Clyde Johnson officiated.

Below: Herbert and his brother, Marvin Coulton 2008.

Herbert &Maxcine Coulton
46 years of marriage

The happy couple!